GOLDEN AGE SPAIN

HENRY KAMEN

M

MACMILLAN
EDUCATION

First published 1988

Published by
MACMILLAN EDUCATION LTD
Houndmills, Basingstoke, Hampshire RG21 2XS
and London
Companies and representatives
throughout the world

Typeset by Wessex Typesetters
(Division of The Eastern Press Ltd.)
Frome, Somerset

Printed in China

British Library Cataloging in Publication Data
Kamen, Henry
Golden age Spain.—(Studies in European
history).
1. Spain, 1469–1714
I. Title   II. Series
946
ISBN 0–333–41930–8

Contents

Editor's Preface

The main purpose of this new series of Macmillan studies is to make available to teacher and student alike developments in a field of history that has become increasingly specialised with the sheer volume of new research and literature now produced. These studies are designed to present the 'state of the debate' on important themes and episodes in European history since the sixteenth century, presented in a clear and critical way by someone who is closely concerned himself with the debate in question.

The studies are not intended to be read as extended bibliographical essays, though each will contain a detailed guide to further reading which will lead students and the general reader quickly to key publications. Each book carries its own interpretation and conclusions, while locating the discussion firmly in the centre of the current issues as historians see them. It is intended that the series will introduce students to historical approaches which are in some cases very new and which, in the normal course of things, would take many years to filter down into the textbooks and school histories. I hope it will demonstrate some of the excitement historians, like scientists, feel as they work away in the vanguard of their subject.

The format of the series conforms closely with that of the companion volumes of studies in economic and social history which has already established a major reputation since its inception in 1968. Both series have an important contribution to make in publicising what it is that historians are doing and in making history more open and accessible. It is vital for history to communicate if it is to survive.

R. J. OVERY

A Note on References

References are cited throughout in brackets according to the numbering in the general bibliography, with page references where necessary indicated by a colon after the bibliography number.

1 Introduction

'The nation, emerging from the sloth and licence of a barbarous age, seemed to prepare like a giant to run its course': such was the vision conjured up in 1837 by the American historian W. H. Prescott when describing the reign of Ferdinand and Isabella; but no sooner had he surveyed the reign than he concluded that the subsequent Habsburg epoch could not be termed a 'golden age', since in comparison it exhibited little more than 'the hectic brilliancy of decay'. On what reign or reigns, then, may a historian of Spain bestow the epithet of 'golden'? It may seem peculiarly inappropriate as a historical term since it suggests a chauvinist optimism that ignores the misery and suffering of the imperial centuries; and its use is now restricted primarily to the realm of literature, where there appears to be agreement that creativity flourished during a well-defined period. However, the chronological limits of the Golden Age have never been clearly specified: for contemporaries it was always an idealised period located in the past, and therefore up to the eighteenth century was normally identified with the Catholic Monarchs; but literary critics of the Enlightenment also judged that the cultural successes of both the sixteenth and seventeenth centuries merited the title of 'golden'. In this book the term is used (with no optimistic intention or any chronological precision) to cover the period from the end of the reign of Henry IV to the early years of that of Philip V, roughly 1470 to 1714, extending from the beginnings of dynastic unity to the beginnings of territorial unity in Spain.

The intention is to offer a short and balanced guide to the current state of scholarship, with an emphasis on recent bibliography and central questions that are the subject of discussion and debate; given the limits on space, some themes will be mentioned only briefly and others not at all. The

1

discussion assumes some familiarity with the historical facts, on which reference should be made to my *Spain 1469–1714. A Society of Conflict* (London & New York, 1984), or, for a more extended treatment, to the volumes by John Lynch[1]; the short study by Bartolomé Bennassar on *Un siècle d'or espagnol* (Paris, 1982) is also well worth consulting.

Since the end of the Franco regime in 1975 there has been a remarkable and sometimes chaotic explosion of historical scholarship within Spain. Prior to that period a handful of notable scholars managed to produce important works of erudition, but an inspirational approach to peninsular studies came mainly from the group of French Hispanists associated with the journal *Annales*. It was with this group, centred in Paris, that the Catalan historian Jaume Vicens Vives in the 1950s came to develop a more positive approach to the writing of his country's history[2]. Since that period, many Spanish scholars have made use in their own work of the research and methods obtaining in other countries, and have thus avoided the danger, which existed for a while in the 1960s, that foreign historians would virtually monopolise their historiography. Nevertheless, given the great attention paid by French scholars to the early modern period, it has been inevitable that the works of Fernand Braudel[3], Pierre Vilar[4], Louis Henry[5] and others should continue to influence approaches to history, even though in practice most historians now look to a broad range of influences, drawn not only from various countries but also from various disciplines.

The explosion of research work has meant considerable advances in our knowledge of certain themes: regional and price history, demographic series, and institutional studies, are among areas which have most benefited. Though there has been an enormous output of highly valuable and pioneering work, most studies are published only in regional journals and presses and it is very difficult to get access to them. The greater attention to localised themes has in the 1980s received enormous stimulus from Spain's autonomous governments, the *autonomías*, which have willingly funded research schemes that emphasise the historic character of the relevant region: as a result, valuable multi-volume histories have been published of Asturias, Andalucia and other areas[6]. The regional

2

approach has the virtue of emphasising traditions and characteristics – in Catalonia and in Galicia, for example – that the previous regime played down, but it also runs the risk of ignoring some of the great unifying factors in Iberian history. In the present outline, which is directed towards the English-speaking reader, due attention will be given to regional issues and to aspects of the monarchy outside the peninsula, but more special emphasis will be placed on factors linking Spain to European trends, since all too often the country is treated as though it were alien to the main features of western civilisation.

Whole volumes have been written about the meaning of the word 'Spain'[7]. In its broadest sense, it referred to the entire peninsula and therefore also included Portugal (the Portuguese poet Camões called Portugal and Spain 'las Españas'); it described no specific political unit and could therefore command the emotional loyalty of provinces that would have been unhappy to submerge their political identity in it. Spain's diversity was in a sense also its strength. The dominant role of Castile in the peninsula, however, led Castile to appropriate the identity of 'Spain', with consequences that continue to affect contemporary culture and politics. For the early modern period, the student needs to remain aware that 'Spain' (like 'Germany' or 'Italy') was little more than a portmanteau word covering a profoundly disunited variety of regions, cultures, governments and consciousnesses; and that though Castilian was the principal Spanish language, many Spaniards – over a quarter of the whole population, if to the Catalans and Portuguese we add a high proportion of Galicians, Basques and Moriscos – did not normally converse in 'Spanish'.

Generations of English-speaking historians have considered Spain worthy of attention mainly in respect of one single theme: the 'decline of Spain'. This theme, which argued that Spain had been powerful and flourishing in the sixteenth century and had then decayed disastrously in the seventeenth, seemed to provide a moral commentary on the inevitable erosion of human pretensions to grandeur[8]. The argument was elaborated by French, Italian, Anglo-Saxon and Spanish historians; the latter, writing particularly in the shadow of the

3

imperial collapse of 1898 (when Spain lost the last vestiges of its American empire), felt that some internal incapacity had blighted Spain's efforts. Since the concept was above all a moral one it never came to acquire any precision, and historians threw in a broad range of ingredients in order to sustain it[9]. The clearest statement of the 'decline' argument in English can be found in Hamilton's 1936 article[10], with a further elaboration in 1963 by Elliott[11]. More recently, it has been argued[12] that the data used to sustain the thesis are so contradictory and faulty that the concept should be discarded; and recent research suggests that though it is in some ways possible to talk of the decay of Spain's empire, there is no useful contribution that the concept of global decline can make to the study of Spain's internal evolution.

Much teaching of Spanish history has concentrated on kings and ministers as a convenient focus of exposition. This is acceptable when dealing with political history, but becomes less useful when broader phenomena, such as culture or the economy, are considered. For this reason the kings of Spain – on whom in any case no studies of quality have been written since the American scholars W. H. Prescott and R. B. Merriman produced their studies on Ferdinand and Isabella (1837) and Philip II (1934) respectively – make little appearance in this essay, but are given due attention where it is relevant; many of the trends discussed here cover several reigns and cannot be pinned down to one historical individual.

The bibliography is highly selective, is normally limited to recent studies (with preference given to work in English and in French, languages which readers from England are likely to know better), and covers only the themes singled out for discussion. Unfamiliar Spanish words are defined in a brief glossary at the end; a fuller glossary can be found in my *Spain 1469–1714*. Perhaps the most valuable guides to recent publications have been produced by Pere Molas, in his survey of the last quarter-century of work in vol. xvii of the *Indice Histórico Español* (Barcelona); and by the same historian and V. Vázquez de Prada in the collective volume *La Historiografía en Occidente desde 1945* (Pamplona, 1985).

2 Spain as a Great Power

'Since God created the world there has been no empire in it as extensive as that of Spain, for from its rising to its setting the sun never ceases to shine for one instant on its lands', was the proud boast in 1655 of the writer Francisco Ugarte de Hermosa. Spanish power was the most obvious reality of European politics for over a century, and its decay in the subsequent century no less obvious. Inevitably, great-power status created hostile foreign attitudes, most of which have been conveniently subsumed under the title of 'the Black Legend'[13]; and in reaction Spanish historiography also adopted attitudes rooted in patriotic sentiment rather than in reality.

The word 'empire' must be used with care. Historians in early modern Spain were unanimous that Ferdinand the Catholic, by the acquisition of territory in Italy and Africa and the New World, 'began the greatness of this immense monarchy' (Fernández Navarrete, 1626); and already by the end of the reign of the Catholic Kings, Nebrija claimed for his country 'the title of Empire'. 'Empire', however, implies conquest and occupation, words which apply correctly only to the African expeditions; by contrast, the possession of Naples and Sicily, secured in 1504, was little more than reversal to a traditional Aragonese control that had been at its peak a mere half century before, under Alfonso the Magnanimous; and Navarre, annexed through dynastic claims in 1512, retained its full autonomy within 'Spain', which itself was a partnership that had grown out of the dynastic union of Castile and Aragon through the marriage of Ferdinand and Isabella. Neither annexation nor union implied conquest: Navarre, Naples and Sicily continued to exist within the monarchy on much the same terms as Aragon, and it would be misleading to regard them as conquered territories. The next decisive phase of 'empire' dates from the multiple accession of Charles V to the territories comprising the Habsburg inheritance (1516–19). However, during the early sixteenth century Spain was in no sense head of that inheritance, exercised little more authority than it had possessed prior to 1516, and remained for all practical purposes at peace with the rest of Christian Europe, participating only as an auxiliary in the wars of Charles V against the Valois rulers of France. From this early period, the various realms associated with Spain were thought of as being a *monarquía*, an association of autonomous units (there were, for example, sovereign parliaments in the Netherlands, Naples, and Sicily) united only by obedience to a common sovereign. In a happy phrase, Pierre Chaunu has referred to this as 'the dynastic Grand Alliance of the seventeen crowns'. Under Charles V, therefore, Spanish power was founded on a fraternal concept of *monarquía*; and in his early years there was strong internal opposition, expressed most openly in the Comunidades, to the idea of empire, which it was felt would make Spain into a junior partner of foreign interests.

However, the appeal of 'empire' grew rapidly. By the late sixteenth century Pedro Salazar de Mendoza argued that the word *monarquía* was no longer appropriate, because 'the *empire* of Spain is twenty times greater than that of the Romans'; and Juan de Salazar in 1619 turned the argument round to say that 'the empire of Spain is rightly called a *monarquía*, if by *monarquía* one means the lordship of almost the whole world'. It has been debated whether there was any 'imperial idea' in Spain at this time; certainly there was a growing number of those who felt that Spain had a destiny to rule, and when they said Spain they usually meant 'Castile'. But though the Italian campaigns of the Great Captain, Gonsalvo de Córdoba, and the seizure of Orán by Cisneros in 1509, demonstrated the vigour of the new Spain of Ferdinand and Isabella, there were few primarily Spanish military or naval achievements in the reign of their successor, the occupation of America being a piecemeal effort carried out by bands of conquistadors and settlers rather than by any official military action, with other enterprises (the victory at Pavia, the capture of Tunis) as joint international ventures in which non-

6

Spaniards were always the majority. Spanish foreign policy under Charles was only one small aspect of the Emperor's global policy and was not the determinant of that policy. Spain certainly gave active help to the Emperor – in Castilian detachments, commanded at one stage by the duke of Alba, and in subsidies, definitively studied by Carande[14] – but was not actively engaged in war. Not surprisingly, some writers came to lament the long peace and the consequent loss of military expertise: Jéronimo de Urrea in 1566 deplored 'the decline of the martial arts in the Spanish infantry of our time'; and in the Council of War in 1562 the 'peace that has reigned here for so many years' was blamed for the defenceless state of the realm.

The rise of Spain as a military and naval power thus occurred principally in the late sixteenth century, as Thompson[15] has demonstrated. The crucial point which emerges from recent work is that Spain, with its small population and weak economy, did not have the resources to create or sustain great-power status. The Romans had been in a similar position, and had solved the problem through naked aggression and annexation of productive areas. Spain, fortunately, as head of 'the dynastic Grand Alliance of the seventeen crowns', could look to its foreign allies for support, offering them many benefits that participation in war might bring: for the elite, honours; for manufacturers and traders, markets and profits; for the common people, employment in the armed forces. Spanish power succeeded in becoming substantial and awesome not because it drew on Spain alone, but because it founded itself on the naval expertise and military manpower of the Genoese and Neapolitans, the weaponry of the Milanese and the Liégeois, the financial backing of Antwerp, the dedication of the crack regiments, the *tercios*, of Castile[16]; by itself Spain could never have battled in the Netherlands or won at Lepanto or mounted the Invincible Armada. This is a significant conclusion that contradicts much traditional historiography, which has treated every exploit of the Golden Age as exclusively 'Spanish'. From the 'Spanish' victory of St Quentin in 1557 (won by a mainly Netherlandish army commanded by the non-Spaniards the Duke of Savoy and the Earl of Egmont) to the 'Spanish' defeat at Rocroy in 1643

7

(lost by a mainly Netherlandish-German army commanded by a Portuguese general), the power of Spain was always determined by the contributions that could be made by its allies. This international nature of the *monarquía* was equally visible at sea: Charles V had no regular naval forces in the Mediterranean until the Genoese fleet opted to join him in 1528, and thereafter the Italians were always the mainstay of Spanish sea-power in southern Europe (at Lepanto in 1571, for example, they supplied two-thirds of the ships and men). Backed by such support, roughly from about 1560 Spain entered on a century of imperialism that ranged over three continents and dragged it into commitments which were soon seen to be disastrous. Why did the government get itself into this situation? Despite accusations by hostile contemporaries, most historians tend to accept the verdict of the Venetian ambassador in 1559 that Philip II aimed 'not to wage war so he can add to his kingdoms, but to wage peace so that he can keep the lands he has'. But 'defensive' policies inevitably became aggressive (the Armada in 1588 and the invasion of France in 1590 are typical examples), and the exercise of extensive military power bred a chauvinism among Castilians that other nations, notably Protestant England, felt they should resist: 'we are hated and abhorred', lamented a Spanish writer in 1594, 'and all because of the wars'. It is interesting that in the circumstances Spain – perhaps uniquely among all 'empires' – never annexed any territory. The occupation of Portugal in 1580 presents no exception: Philip was the direct heir, his candidature was approved by the Portuguese Cortes, and he adhered faithfully to his undertaking to keep the governments of Portugal and Castile completely separate.

Thanks to the survival of documentation, the financial implications of war during the 'imperial century', 1560–1660, have been studied in detail. It has become clear that Spain was dragged into foreign commitments that came to absorb the bulk of state revenue: *juro* repayments, for loans made largely to the war effort, absorbed by the end of Charles V's reign in 1556 some 68 per cent of normal Castilian revenue; by 1565 the figure was up to 84 per cent, and by the end of Philip's reign in 1598 the total *juro* debt was nearly eight times that of annual revenue. The cost of imperialism was clearly

8

ruinous: in 1634, under Olivares, over 93 per cent of expenditure was earmarked for foreign policy. Felipe Ruiz Martín concludes that 'war in the sixteenth century cut short the positive evolution of Spain by absorbing resources which would normally have served to increase production. . . . The proliferation of *juros* checked growth. . . . War, for Spain, had a decisive influence on the economic process'[17].

Though much research exists on finances, relatively little has been done on the mechanics of Spanish imperialism, and it is still unclear what part Spanish resources played in relation to those of other countries; the only general discussion of this question is the perceptive essay by Stradling[18]. On questions of manpower, Parker has convincingly studied the military relationship between the peninsula and the Netherlands, and in the process has given us splendid insight into the mechanics of the sixteenth-century army in Flanders[19]. Thompson has also looked at recruitment during the same period, but for the entire seventeenth century we remain in the dark about the recruitment, officering and administration of the Spanish forces, and recent studies, such as that by Elliott on the early century[25], have disappointingly omitted these crucial themes; we only know that by the War of Succession[20] the army was no match for its enemies, and relied heavily on foreigners as general officers. *If* there was a deterioration – the so-called 'decline' – how and when did it occur? The same question may be posed for the naval forces of the crown: there are useful general surveys, but no historian has yet approached the subject in detail. Spain's capability in shipbuilding is not in doubt: well into the late seventeenth century, the epoch of alleged decline, a sample of 239 vessels used in the American trade shows that only 37 per cent were foreign-built, the rest being constructed either in America or in Spain, mainly in Basque shipyards. On the supply of war-materials, there is a key study[21] of the iron industry of northern Spain, but no adequate information about armaments, gunpowder, and related items has yet emerged, leaving one to suspect that Spain had little. This is not wholly surprising, since Spain's wars tended to be fought abroad, not at home, and it was more sensible to supply the army of Flanders from the more industrialised Netherlands and Liège, and the army of Milan from Milan itself. The peninsula, so easily invaded during the War of Succession, was just as defenceless over a century earlier, when the English in 1596 captured and held Cadiz for three weeks. The evidence thus suggests not so much a decline as a *failure* right from the start, to build up the defences of the peninsula.

The role of Milan and Italy is touched on only marginally in all the literature and urgently needs study in itself. Since Renaissance times, Italy had been the key to European power and hence the theatre of some of Charles V's most important campaigns. By granting Milan to his son Philip in 1540, the Emperor made sure that the Spanish *monarquía* would hold a strategic prize that thereafter became essential to its survival, for three main reasons: it dominated northern Italy and therefore restricted Venetian, papal and French pretensions; it supplied two key routes to northern Europe, through the 'Spanish road' and through the Valtelline; and it drew on important Italian manpower, armament and banking resources, as well as the naval resources of Genoa. Spain's domination of northern Italy remained at all times the highest priority of Spanish imperial policy, and inevitably invited French intervention in the early seventeenth century, when Olivares made the mistake of pressing Spanish interests to the point of war (1628) over the Mantuan succession[25].

The current decline of interest in diplomatic history has meant that we still do not know enough about the formation of policy and about public opinion, and most of our assumptions about Spanish foreign policy have remained unchanged over the past century. Despite a pioneering study by Mattingly on diplomacy under Ferdinand the Catholic[22], none of the great career diplomats of the imperial age has been studied in depth (though several studies of lesser figures exist). Of political personalites in the late sixteenth century, only Cardinal Granvelle has received the detailed attention required[23]. From a study of Spanish intervention in the French religious wars[24] and the exposition by Elliott on Olivares' entry into the Thirty Years War[25] it appears that Spain, while not actively expansionist, was drawn into conflicts by the obvious need to protect its interests, so that it would be unjust to consider its policies as uniformly aggressive. By

10

the same token, priorities were never exclusively ideological, and Spain seldom acted as the secular arm of the Counter Reformation; in respect of the papacy, the essay by Lynch puts relations in perspective[26], making it clear that for all the identity of religious aims the political objectives of Philip II never coincided with those of the pope. And yet there was an indubitable chauvinism about Spain's role, with its insistence on preserving honour and *reputación*, that infuriated other Europeans. This negative image abroad, cultivated even by allies of the crown such as Italians and Belgians, helped to perpetuate the Black Legend well into the epoch of the Thirty Years War, and does scant justice to the real differences of opinion that always existed among Spaniards. State documents leave no doubt that there were often quite fundamental disagreements among the policy-makers, though there is little evidence to justify, for example, the old and simplistic picture of two rival policy factions under Philip II, one of the duke of Alba which favoured a 'ruthless' solution to imperial affairs and the other of the prince of Eboli which favoured 'negotiation'. In practice, issues were never seen in such stark 'war' and 'peace' terms. Alba, like any professional soldier, wanted a quick, clean military solution; he thought that this was possible in Flanders just as he later thought it was not possible in England and so opposed the 'war' policy of Granvelle and those who counselled an invasion[27].

A generation of war under Philip II was enough to excite strong reaction, and the subsequent government was in tune with public opinion when it sought peace. The Netherlands revolt was Spain's Vietnam, sucking the money and lives of the interventionists, and like Vietnam it provoked a passionate nation-wide debate: 'no one knows', wrote the Jesuit Juan de Mariana in 1609, 'when this war will end, our losses have been great and the humiliation greater.' Maravall has made a short study of the controversy and has identified it in some measure as opposition to the government[28]. The war, however, culminating as it did with the independence of the Dutch in 1648, had other profound and long-term reverberations: it brought to some a disenchantment with the dream of empire, and sparked off the literature of disillusion produced by *arbitristas* within Castile. As early as 1598 Alamos de

11

Barrientos claimed to see 'our realms defenceless, infested, invaded; the Mediterranean and Atlantic lorded over by the enemy; the Spanish nation worn out, prostrate, discontented and disfavoured; *reputación* and honour laid low'. Such exaggerations were to become the stock-in-trade of subsequent commentators. A generation later, in 1624, an official of the Council of the Indies asked the question, 'Why should we pursue a ruinous war that has gone on for sixty-six years, and is leading us to destruction?' The need to disengage from the whole of the Netherlands without prejudicing imperial security came to be a constant objective of the policy-makers, particularly after 1648.

Though the peace party was influential in Madrid at the turn of the century and under Lerma[29], Spain's professional diplomats – Osuna in Naples and Oñate in Vienna, for example – sounded alarm signals at the continuing threat to Spanish interests from the Dutch, whose fleets had used the Twelve Years Truce to make massive incursions into Portuguese and Spanish territory overseas, and whose agents were active throughout Protestant Europe as well as in Venice and in Bohemia. The drift into conflict with the expiry of the Truce in 1621 formed part of the general European conflagration known as the Thirty Years War[30]; what has become clearer with recent research is that the entire first phase of the war, up to about 1630, and including within it major events such as the occupation of the Palatinate, the Mantuan venture, and the plan for a Baltic fleet[31], was centred round the epic struggle between the United Provinces and Spain[32], a struggle which saw Spain's forces committed on every European front and which terminated in dismal and unquestionable failure, leading Olivares to grieve that 'neither in Flanders nor in Italy have we done anything except lose *reputación*'. The opening of hostilities with France in 1635 was not at first traumatic, since France had little military experience and would soon be preoccupied with its domestic troubles in the Fronde; but the strains imposed on the creaking *monarquía* by war, economic crisis, and French-inspired conspiracies among the elites of Catalonia, Portugal and Naples, brought the whole structure to its knees.

Most surveys of foreign policy terminate with the Peace of

12

Westphalia in 1648 and that of the Pyrenees in 1659. Stradling has argued with reason that the war effort of these decades cannot be written off simply by citing the defeat at Rocroi (1643), and that in 1652 there was an impressive display of strength with the recapture, on three distinct fronts, of Barcelona, Dunkirk and Casale[18]. Though the truly great territorial losses were still to come, there can be little argument that after 1660 Spain had lost any real capacity to maintain its international position and was truly 'in decline': the 'imperial century' simply ran out of steam. Subsequent decades, which have been tentatively surveyed[33] but which merit detailed research, saw many Spanish statesmen reverting to the traditional Mediterranean-based policies that had predated the great age of empire; some evidence of this is given in the proposal, first made by Mazarin and then warmly supported in Spain, for the surrender to France of the southern Netherlands in exchange for the provinces of Catalonia lost in 1659. The most astonishing feature of the post-1648 period, however, was the diplomatic revolution by which Spain entered into a close alliance with the Dutch, who were needed for the primary purpose of defending the southern Netherlands and restraining the aggression of Louis XIV; the rapprochement attained its apogee in the 1670s with the admission of Dutch garrisons into Spanish fortresses in Flanders and the joint manoeuvres of the Dutch and Spanish fleets in the Mediterranean, culminating in the Protestant admiral De Ruyter giving his life in battle in 1676 for the defence of Catholic Spain.

We have seen that Spain's imperial role was made possible only by the joint resources of several countries. It followed ineluctably that those countries soon resented the burden imposed on them, and saw the Spanish connection as a yoke to be thrown off. Already under Charles V there were complaints of the rising cost of the wars in Germany and the Mediterranean: in the Netherlands special taxation rose steeply between the 1530s and the 1560s[34]. The Low Countries, however, were of great strategic and economic value to Spain, whose government felt it should take a hard line when presented with protests: the result was a rapid slide into a war of repression that devoured Spanish military

13

resources for three-quarters of a century. Although the southern Netherlands (Belgium) remained allied to Spain (1579–1713), there too the same protests continued to be made[35]. In Italy the accumulated burden of heavy taxation and Spanish control provoked important rebellions in Naples (1647)[36] and in Messina (1674)[37]. These, considered together with the peninsular rebellions of 1640, demonstrate that the *monarquía* was breaking apart because of unequal burdens imposed by the imperial programme of Castile.

It was the feeling of dissatisfaction that eventually persuaded the United Provinces, Belgium, Naples and other realms, to sever their link with Spain. Similar motives had impelled the Catalans[38] and Portuguese in 1640 (to say nothing of the abortive plots in Andalucia and in Aragon). However, some Castilians, like Fernández de Navarrete and Olivares, saw the problem in quite a different light: to them it appeared that the weakness of the *monarquía* derived precisely from the excessive autonomy of each constituent realm, and that Castile alone had been shouldering the burden of empire for the preceding two generations. Each side of the argument was in some measure correct. Naples, the Netherlands, and Portugal were fully sovereign states, with their own separate parliaments, institutions, and laws: all they shared in common was their king, and it was repugnant to them that their interests should always be subordinated to those of Castile. Olivares, for his part, felt that this loose federation of states should be turned into a real fusion of resources. It was not a crazy dream: his contemporary, the Italian priest Campanella, who spent twenty years in a Spanish prison in Naples, also felt that a truly powerful empire could be based on Spain, with all nationalities serving equally in it, Portuguese for example in Castile and Castilians in Portugal. But, in addition to the constant particularism of each state, there were other reasons which by the early seventeenth century helped to undermine Spanish power.

The fundamental fact is that Castile's inadequate manpower and industrial resources (see Chapter 3) made it ill-equipped to sustain an imperial programme for long; in this it had an exact parallel in seventeenth-century Sweden. At most, the country might manage to finance a programme that was being

14

serviced by its allies, which is what in effect happened under Philip II, with Castile paying the bills but its allies supplying the men and the munitions. Catastrophic state debt, however, made it impossible to go on. The obligations of imperial power, moreover, forced Spain to over-extend its commitments: during the Thirty Years War it had fighting units in Bohemia, Germany, Belgium, and Italy, with naval forces in Brazil and America and defensive units in north Africa, Portugal and Spain (Philip IV in a burst of misinformed optimism in 1625 declared that he had some 800,000 men under arms throughout the war theatres, and this was before the outbreak of hostilities with France). Finally, the persistent pressure of enemy powers, principally the Dutch up to 1648 and the French after the declaration of war in 1635, put intolerable strains on the overburdened Spanish military machine. In the opening years of the seventeenth century, Spanish ministers recognised the seriousness of the strength arrayed against them: 'we cannot by force of arms reduce those provinces', commented Baltasar de Zúñiga in 1619, referring to the Dutch; by 1635, despite the optimism of Olivares, many approached the conflict against France with dismay. In the circumstances, it may be said that the *rise* of imperial power from the 1560s was what directly precipitated decline: rise and decay were alternate faces of the same phenomenon, and there was nothing mysterious about the collapse of Spanish hegemony in Europe by about 1660, when the century of preponderance turned full circle.

The collapse of Spanish power in the western world has been surveyed by Hussey[39] and, within the context of Italy, by Alcalá-Zamora[40]. When the War of Succession came in 1702, the government's inability to fight a war on home soil was demonstrated clearly by its heavy reliance on foreign, mainly French troops, and by its almost total reliance on France for basic supplies (armaments, uniforms)[20]. This time there was a determination to be rid of the Habsburg inheritance, and the Spanish Netherlands were placed firmly in the hands of France. The poverty of Spain's war potential, however, was apparently no graver in 1705 than in 1605, so that the idea of a 'decline' is unhelpful: the likely situation was that between these dates Spain had taken only limited

15

steps to enhance its service industries (munitions, gunpowder etc), and was happy to draw on the resources of its allies in the *monarquía*. Moreover, while other nations (particularly the France of Louvois) were modernising and *nationalising* their armies, Spain continued to rely on classic and well-tried methods that had helped its crack regiments, the *tercios*, dominate the battlefields of the early seventeenth century, but proved unsuitable in the conditions of the late century, when the enemy was using new weapons and new techniques. Most surprising of all for a country which relied so heavily on communications, the Spain that had been able to muster enormous armadas in cases of emergency never succeeded in establishing a good regular navy, and throughout the seventeenth century the clearest index to the crumbling of its hegemony is the series of naval defeats it suffered at the hands of the Dutch (from the plate fleet in 1628 to the Downs in 1639), the English (from Drake's sacking of Santo Domingo in 1585 to Blake's attack on the plate fleet in 1657), and the French (from Guetaria in 1638 to the bombardment of Barcelona and Alicante in 1691).

No consideration of Spain's imperial position can omit America. The conquest of the Indians of the New World has been among the most celebrated accomplishments of the Spanish people, and has strengthened the image of great imperial power. It must be remembered, however, that no official military or naval forces were involved in these conquests of the early sixteenth century, which were undertaken mainly by groups of adventurers; and that the high American civilisations were overthrown more by internal weaknesses than by the superior might of the conquerors. In what is still the best study of the subject[41], W. H. Prescott stated that 'the Aztec monarchy fell by the hands of its own subjects'; though in the case of the Incas such a judgment must be tempered by the fact that resistance continued for a further generation[42]. Thereafter, America seemed for a while to be the jewel in the crown of Castile: it sent bullion and precious goods to Spain, and the trade stimulated Spanish industry and agriculture; what is more, the government did not have to spend money on a military presence, since the settlers did their own policing. However, in practical terms America contributed little to

16

Spanish imperial strength; naval costs continued to increase, and defence needs against foreign marauders in the Caribbean consumed the greater part of the income from bullion and taxes, so that the Castilian treasury for most of the seventeenth century discounted America as a serious contributor of income[43].

3 The Peninsular Economy

In no area of Spain's past has so much work been done recently as on its economic history; this has meant that some classic works, such as Vicens Vives' *Economic History of Spain* (1958), have been rapidly superseded. However, progress is very uneven; some themes, such as family structure, are only just beginning to be studied, and others, such as foreign trade, remain almost totally neglected. We shall attempt here to look at questions both of historical development and of economic structure.

In the preceding chapter it was emphasised that early modern Spain was a poor country with no capacity to sustain an imperial programme out of its own resources. How then did it manage to survive? In simple terms, it had a phase of modest prosperity in the sixteenth century: industry expanded, population increased, output rose. This prosperity was not of course exclusively self-generated; the whole European economy was in a phase of expansion during the same period. There were aspects of the Spanish boom which help to clarify its later development and which remind us that the country must constantly be viewed within its international context if we are to understand it. This is particularly true of the price rise. Though Spain is thought of as the classic country of the 'price revolution', which Hamilton in a seminal work[44] attributed mainly to the import of American bullion, it is now clear that all European countries underwent the same process, which had multiple causes associated with population increase and agrarian change; in the peninsula, nonetheless, the situation was made worse by an adverse trade balance, which raised foreign demand for bullion and thus inflated internal prices. There was, moreover, a secondary inflation, provoked by monetary debasement in the early seventeenth century, which continued to produce high prices in Spain when they were

19

falling in the rest of Europe; this was intimately tied to the previous factor, since the issue of coin with a lower bullion content (i.e. debasement) was the only alternative facing a nation that exported most of its precious metals either for trade or for government military costs. The situation improved after the mid-seventeenth century, when the value of bullion began to fall (it was superfluous to the European trade process and vast quantitites were exported to Asia[45]), thus making it possible for Castile in the late century (by the decrees of 1680 and 1686) to stabilise its currency without calling on further resources[46].

The evolution of population in Spain was likewise closely related to European trends. Continuous series for baptisms, marriages and burials in parish records start roughly from the mid-sixteenth century, when the Council of Trent enjoined parish priests to keep these statistics, but in a few cases data can be found from the early century. Diligent work in the records has now produced for Spain perhaps the largest number of continuous series available for any European country: and as a result there can be little dispute over the main pattern observable in most of the peninsula[47]: a slow increase from the late fifteenth into the early sixteenth century, with a marked and sometimes dramatic expansion in the central decades of the century to about 1580, then a steep fall from about 1590 to about 1650, and a slow recovery from 1660 into the early eighteenth century. The mid-sixteenth century expansion can be identified concretely in Old Castile with the commercial boom of those years in towns such as Segovia and Valladolid[48], and in Seville with the expansion of American trade[49]. Analysis of the 1591 tax-paying population (the *pecheros*) throughout Castile suggests that between 1528 and that date numbers rose by about 50 per cent, with an annual growth rate of 0.61 per cent[50]. In some towns the increase was striking, particularly in the south and in Galicia. The decline after 1590 can be identified in Old Castile with the decay of the fairs of Medina del Campo[51], and in New Castile with the rapid decline of Toledo[52] as Madrid rose to prominence; the period was also notable for several important epidemics which had a highly negative impact on the heartland of Spain[53]. The demographic recovery after

1660, confirmed in recent studies[54], was slow and continued despite several negative factors.

To this general picture, some important modifications must be made. Nadal, Pérez Moreda and others distinguish between a pattern for 'interior' or peninsular Spain, and another for the periphery or coastal Spain, with recovery occurring earlier in the coastal areas. This division, however, leaves out of consideration the major variant of the north-west, particularly Galicia and Asturias, where the expansion of the sixteenth century was muted, but by contrast the seventeenth in its entirety was one of marked expansion, and only from the 1690s into the eighteenth century was there a sharp demographic reverse[55]. We should also bear in mind that, in Valencia at least, growth rates for Moriscos (one-third of the population) were higher than those for Christians. Thus the great complexity of demographic development in the peninsula makes it difficult to posit one single pattern. In rounded terms, the population of Spain (including the Balearic Islands but excluding the Canaries and Portugal) probably rose from about 5.25 million in the 1480s to a ceiling of about 8 million in the late sixteenth century, remaining after the depression period at around 7 million until the later decades of the eighteenth century.

In general, Spain coincides with European trends of growth in the sixteenth century and deceleration in the early seventeenth. Expansion in the peninsula in the early sixteenth century was helped by the absence of any major epidemics, and by the lack of foreign wars. The middle years of the century thus show considerable evidence of economic growth, with industrial and agricultural expansion, a boom in trade and finance, and urban construction. Molinié-Bertrand has posited a 78 per cent increase in the population of New Castile between 1528 and 1591, the steepest increase coming after 1560; in Jaén, further south, the increase was also high, at 75.5 per cent[50]. From the late century, however, negative signs increased: there were epidemics, grain shortages, and the beginning of direct involvement in military action against the Turks and the Dutch. The symptoms of recession were various, and could be identified all over Europe, but they were clearly visible in many key sectors of the Spanish

21

economy, as Casey has lucidly shown[56]. It is possible too that emigration to America had an adverse effect, though the numbers involved appear not to have been of crisis proportions: the official figures have been analysed[65] but merit little confidence, and historians have had to resort to estimates. From the 1580s, parish records show a definite downswing in birth figures. In most of Spain, the demographic crisis appears to have lasted for two generations, with further desolation wreaked by the great epidemics of 1596–1602 and 1647–54. The population levels fell so sharply that they were not regained until the middle years of the eighteenth century; and contemporaries continued for generations to make wildly exaggerated claims about the crisis, statistical accuracy not being one of the virtues of the age. There was much introspective pessimism[57], particularly when writers saw stagnation within and military defeat abroad; it is this epoch that many contemporaries and some historians have looked upon as the apogee of 'decline'. A slightly different demographic pattern can be observed on the Mediterranean coast: in Catalonia, it appears that population rose in the early sixteenth century by only 20 per cent, but the rate accelerated to about 75 per cent between the 1550s and the 1620s, in which increase a major role has been attributed by Nadal and Giralt to the factor of French immigration[58] (in the parish of Sant Just in Barcelona in 1576–1625 some 23 per cent of men getting married were French); thereafter no major interruption appears to have occurred until the crisis of the 1640 rebellion and the serious epidemic of 1654. The major variation in north-west Spain, observed in several studies[59], has been explicitly attributed to the introduction of maize, which is mentioned further below.

The virtually total absence of studies of family structure in early modern Spain means that we know little about the internal evolution of population, and the best that we can achieve is a series of snapshots rather than a moving film. The snapshots that have been most analysed are official censuses made in Castile in 1561[60] and 1591[50], but data from regional archives are also beginning to be explored, and coincide in offering us various profiles of the population of Castile in terms of wealth and profession. Work on the parish records has given further insight into family structure in the peninsula. The mean age of first marriage for women (a crucial determinant of fertility) has been shown to be about 20 years in the Algarve, Valladolid, Cuenca and Mallorca around the mid-sixteenth century; in the mid-seventeenth in the Catalan lands (Gerona, Barcelona) and in parts of Valencia (Guadalest, Alicante) there are cases of the age rising to 22, but against this we must balance the various Morisco communities of the period (Extremadura, Valencia) where the mean age varied from 20 down to 18 years[61]. The notably low age of female marriage, in contrast to the standard west European pattern where the mean age of female first marriage was 24 years, has led Casey[62] to suggest that the Spanish demographic pattern was basically non-European. However, it is also certain that in a substantial part of the peninsula, specifically the north-west including Galicia and northern Portugal, female first marriage in the seventeenth century occurred at about 27 years, bringing this area more into line with western Europe; in the eighteenth century the pattern was maintained, with late marriage as a clear feature of the north-west, including Cantabria and the Basque Provinces. It has been argued that the north-west had a 'developed' or modern pattern, and that the centre and south had an 'archaic' or mediaeval model which was evolving towards the west European model. The significance of these peninsular patterns, which in any case need to be set within a broader context (low age of marriage can also be found in Italy at this period), remains unclear as long as we continue to have little information about other variables. It seems, for example, that the capacity of the low marriage age in Spain to replace population lost by epidemics must have been restricted by the high level of abstinence from marriage, an abstinence dictated either by choice (religion) or economic status (servant girls) or early widowhood (this would affect the frequency of second marriages). Molinié-Bertrand states that in the 1590s 'single women, either widows or celibate, constituted between 20 per cent and 30 per cent of the population of Castilian cities'. The profile suggested by this author on the basis of the 1591 census is that the Castilian woman married at about 18 years, had her first child after about a year, and bore her last child at the age of 35: if this can be confirmed, it offers a period of fertility – some seventeen years – not very different from the fifteen years common in the west European pattern. However, the high level of celibacy (notably higher than the 20 per cent maximum posited by Hajnal for western Europe), and the high rate of infant mortality, resulted in inadequate population replacement and therefore in a negative demographic tendency, whose duration still needs to be squared with other population data.

Among the major factors that depleted population were epidemics, emigration and war. Because epidemics prior to the seventeenth century are often poorly documented, it is difficult either to date them or measure their intensity. Detailed work has been done for Castile on outbreaks of the early modern period[53], and on those of the late sixteenth century[63], with surveys of those of 1647–54[64] and of 1676–85[54]. There can be no doubt that the epidemics intensified mortality greatly; over one million people died in the seventeenth-century epidemics alone, with death rates sometimes at ten times the normal. In broader perspective, we must note that a mortality crisis of possibly even worse proportions was occurring in Italy at the same period, so the misfortunes of Spain should be seen not in isolation but as part of a general demographic collapse in the Mediterranean.

Spain's population was also subject to attrition through emigration. Internal emigration was neutral in impact: it occurred when men moved in search of seasonal labour, and to these movements we must add that of foreign workers, mostly southern French, who came into the country in great numbers during the entire early modern period and normally returned home after the harvest season. It seems that the famous seasonal migration to Andalucia of Galician workers only began in the 1690s and became notable in the mid-eighteenth century, but lack of sources for the earlier period may obscure its existence then[55]. External emigration was certainly negative in impact: the flow of registered as well as illegal emigrants to the New World may have totalled 250,000 for the whole sixteenth century, and substantially less for the seventeenth[65], but lack of reliable data makes it difficult to consider the question properly. The two great cultural

24

expulsions of the period – that of the Jews in 1492 and that of the Moriscos in 1609–14 – were unique of their kind, and require some comment. Figures upwards of 150,000 have usually been suggested for the Jews expelled; but when we bear in mind that the decree aimed at *conversion* rather than expulsion, that the Jews were in any case a tiny minority after the forced conversions of the previous century, and that very many returned to Spain after leaving it in the 1490s, it seems acceptable to suggest that the real total emigration was not more than about 50,000[66], and that the economic repercussions were negligible. The Morisco expulsions, on the other hand, cannot be played down: some 300,000 Spaniards were driven from their homeland, representing one-third of the population of Valencia and one-fifth that of Aragon, and the short-term consequences were serious in some areas[67]; but the Moriscos themselves had been declining both in population and in their economic contribution to their land-lords[68], so that the overall impact on the Christian economy was not uniformly disastrous, and many nobles were able to accept the expulsions without regret.

Since Spain tended to fight its wars abroad rather than at home, their demographic impact must be measured principally in terms of the emigration of soldiers. Given that the 'Spanish' army was made up primarily of non-Spaniards, the numbers involved were not large; it must also be remembered that by their constitutions the *fuero* realms sent few men abroad, so that the burden fell mainly on Castile. Under Philip II about 9,000 men a year were recruited from Spain; in crisis years the totals could double. One may speculate that the absence of many young men from their homes from the 1570s onwards contributed to the fall in the domestic birth rate: this appears to have been the result in Cáceres[69]. Hostilities within Spain normally affected only the Moriscos (the Granada wars of 1569–70) but the country also suffered two important internal wars: that against Portugal (1640–68), which had profound consequences on Extremadura[54], and the War of Succession[20]. Even at the time, commentators were aware that Spanish imperialism was exacting a heavy price of Castile's limited population.

The economy of pre-industrial Europe was overwhelmingly agricultural, and a basic guide to economic progress in Spain

25

would be the measurement of agrarian productivity. The most common method of doing this has been to use tithe returns as a basis; since tithes were normally a tenth of produce, the data would allow an accurate estimate of the full harvest to be made. From the many useful studies that have been made[48; 70], it can be seen that the curve for production generally coincides with the curve for population. In the archbishopric of Toledo, a territory that included most of New Castile, cereal production rose steadily from 1460 to 1560, reaching its zenith in the period 1560–80; thereafter, there was a decline until the decade 1640–50, followed by stagnation or by a slow recovery into the late seventeenth century[71]. This general outline could also be found in other areas such as Catalonia and the Basque country, but with significant differences for the seventeenth century. In Catalonia, for example, there was a crisis of agrarian production and a decline in seigneurial returns from the 1620s into the 1660s, a problem aggravated no doubt by the civil conflicts. In general terms, then, the sixteenth century was one of expanding output and the early seventeenth one of crisis. Once again, we must note the major exception of the north-west: the introduction of maize here helped to stabilise cereal output and keep population levels high. In Asturias already by 1617 maize was 'the sustenance of the poor people', thus preceding by over a decade its adoption in Galicia[72], and production remained high throughout the seventeenth century, thus helping to rescue the north-west from the economic crisis of the rest of the peninsula.

Given the great variety of climate and land use in the peninsula it is obvious that there were significant differences everywhere. We must first of all ask: was there really an increase in *production* in the sixteenth century? There can be little doubt that no qualitative innovations in technique occurred, and Spanish literature on the topic was – apart from Gabriel Alonso de Herrera's best-seller *Agricultura General* (1513) – sparse. Yield ratios, that is, the proportion of grain reaped to grain sown, remained among the lowest in western Europe, in Old Castile at about 4:1 in wheat, though higher rates can be found elsewhere. Thus if there was higher output it came about exclusively because more land was put under the plough: towns encroached on their common lands, individuals usurped or bought (from a penurious crown) public royal lands (*baldíos*)[73], cities disputed with the Mesta over rights to pasture. None of this was enough to feed the growing population satisfactorily, but thanks to regular imports, particularly from Sicily, Spain seems to have had no food riots before the early seventeenth century. Second, did the undoubted fall in production in the subsequent period (in Segovia wheat output fell by 30 per cent between the 1580s and 1640[48]) represent a real decline in food supplies? The answer is almost certainly 'no': output seems to have been adjusted to fit demand from a smaller population. In the village of Torrejoncillo wheat output between 1630 and 1684 fell by over 50 per cent, but the supply per household remained constant since the population had also shrunk[54]. Gonzalo Anés has argued with good reason that the depression had positive aspects which helped to overcome the crisis: 'where population decline meant a shrinkage of arable, more pasture became available to feed more livestock. With cultivation reduced to only the best lands, a rise in output per unit sown was an inevitable consequence. The decrease in population guaranteed a proportionally higher return for each worker, and in these areas agricultural surpluses became possible'[74]. Third, there were important changes in the types of *crop sown*. The most remarkable case is the north-west, where the introduction of maize from the 1630s revolutionised living standards, and in Galicia by the late century represented over three-fourths of all cereals. With a higher yield ratio of up to 50:1, and a shorter vegetative cycle which left the land free for other use, maize became the salvation of the poor peasantry. In other parts of Spain, too, changes occurred. The expulsion of the Moriscos, who were for the most part not wheat-eating, allowed land to come back into wheat production for the Christian population. In some areas the higher yield ratio of non-wheat cereals encouraged farmers to shift their crop emphasis (mainly to barley) so as to get more grain, which in any case was desired for feeding livestock: in parts of Andalucia the increase in barley output in the late seventeenth century was four times greater than in wheat. Finally, we know that the availability of land, as wheat production shrank, encouraged

27

a move to *viticulture*; it was a fair commercial decision, but strongly denounced by those who, like the official Caxa de Leruela (1631), felt that wheat (for human mouths) should have priority.

The crucial importance of agriculture, which apart from a brief pioneering essay by Viñas y Mey[75] remained largely neglected, has begun to attract the attention of historians. Jesús García Fernández has done some pioneering work on systems of cultivation[76] and Vassberg has returned to the debate, popularised by a past generation of scholars such as Joaquín Costa, over the importance of communal exploitation of holdings[77]; he has also contributed usefully to the very complex discussion over the problems of the Castilian economy. Although we now have some fine surveys of the evolution of the rural economy, especially in its ascendant phase[78], there are differing views about why problems arose: Vassberg sums up many opinions when he says that 'the real problem was not meteorological but human: poverty was the result of man-made institutions that were inefficient, and that did not permit the proper utilization of resources'. Among the reasons offered by historians for this situation are: inequitable land-distribution, the preference of the communal system for antiquated techniques of exploitation (such as rotation methods and use of mules), the difficulty of obtaining cash or credit for investment in the soil (hence the increase in rural debt, provoked by the use of the *censo*), and the burden of rents and taxes. Discussion on all these points is necessarily open-ended, since there were immense variations throughout the peninsula. The situation of the peasant could change substantially, for example, depending on whose jurisdiction he fell under. In some parts of Aragon and in post-Morisco Valencia[62] the dependence of peasants on the lords was heavy; but even in free Castile, as Salomon has argued[79], burdens depressed the producing classes. It has been usual to talk of a freer peasantry in Catalonia after the Sentence of Guadalupe of 1486, but there too the changes were not favourable[80] and the lot of the poorer peasants worsened. Thus the position of the rural classes in early modern Spain seems to have been aggravated on one hand by an unprogressive agricultural system, on the other by a restricting social environment: this situation, of course, was common throughout southern Europe and the Mediterranean.

The agrarian crisis, when it came after the 1580s, could be seen in: a fall in wheat production (by at least a third, and often much more); a decline in rental income (in Segovia landlords complained of falls of 50 per cent); a shrinkage of arable; a decrease in livestock (the flocks of the Mesta, Klein shows, fell from some three million head in the sixteenth century to two million in the seventeenth); and a levelling-off in commodity and food prices, which however maintained their upward trend because of monetary inflation. The contraction also occurred in other countries, but the impact on Spain was arguably more severe, with no evidence that structural changes occurred as a result of the crisis, leading Casey to conclude that 'Spain's peculiar failure was an inability to complete the transition to a more urbanised economy'[56], a transition that nations in northern Europe were successfully making.

The pastoral economy has been little studied. Livestock (cattle, sheep, pigs, goats) was crucial to the rural economy; sheep were particularly important, being the mainstay of the cottage and textile industry (in its main centres at Segovia, Toledo, and Cuenca), and also of the export trade; there was therefore good reason to maintain extensive pasture. However, a long historiographical tradition dating from the eighteenth century has given a continuously bad press to the sheepowners' guild, the Mesta[81], by attributing many of the failings of the economy to the pastoral interest. Vassberg summarises the findings of modern scholarship when he states that 'some historians have concluded that early modern Spanish agriculture was ruined by depredations of migratory flocks. That is simply not true'[77].

Given the predominance of the agrarian sector in all pre-industrial economies, it is obvious that the industrial sector was small. In Spain this was particularly so, both because of a lack of resources and because the markets were small and regionalised in a country which had no unified political structure. Only fragmentary information is available on pre-eighteenth century industry, but it appears that the main textile areas in the mid-sixteenth century were Segovia (the most important for woollens), Granada (silk), Toledo (silk and woollens) and Cuenca (woollens). In line with demographic growth and agricultural expansion in the late fifteenth century there appears to have been a notable increase in textile output, on the evidence from Cuenca[82]. Side by side with this domestic industry, however, there had existed since the later Middle Ages an active export trade of quality wool (the merino sheep) and silk from Granada. Well into the sixteenth century the right of domestic manufacturers to at least a third of raw materials was guaranteed by public authority. By then, however, the international economic situation had changed, and foreigners who bought Spanish raw materials were turning them into quality manufactured goods and sending these back into Spain at competitive prices. Spain's soaring inflation, and consequent higher production costs, helped to make the foreign textiles relatively cheaper; moreover, foreign manufacturers were even more encouraged to export to Spain by the possibility of being paid in American bullion. Thus Spain's domestic industry faced difficult times. Some internal developments made the situation worse: in Granada, for example, the old Moorish textile industry was slowly crushed by non-Morisco speculators who cornered raw silk production and sought good prices from foreign buyers. Commentators and members of the Cortes, particularly in the seventeenth century, asked for protectionist measures such as a ban on the export of bullion and of raw materials, but these were unrealistic demands that would also have had negative effects on Spain. The textile industry had a moment of glory in the boom of the sixteenth century, when production at Segovia by 1585 attained levels comparable to famous centres such as Florence[48], but soon many merchants were getting better returns from exporting wool than from selling it to Spanish factories. Figures for cloth production tell plainly the sad story of a fragile domestic textile industry that recovered slightly during the early eighteenth century but in general remained depressed until the nineteenth.)

The wool trade was fundamental and played a key role in the growth of Spain's financial market, centred during the early sixteenth century in the northern towns of Burgos and Medina del Campo, with good access to the trading ports of

Bilbao and Santander[83]. Since foreign merchants were those primarily interested in the trade, the business life of these towns had a truly cosmopolitan air, and thanks to Lapeyre's studies of the Ruiz family[84] we know a good deal about the functioning and difficulties of trade at that time. The decay of the fairs of northern Castile after the 1570s, provoked to a great extent by the disturbances in the important market of the Netherlands, was the prelude to a restructuring of the Castilian economy, for precisely at this period large sections of the peninsula were benefiting from the discovery of America[85]. The middle years of the sixteenth century were thus a boom period in which the success story of the Castilian fairs overlapped with the new wealth of Seville and Andalucia, bringing a sensation of well-being to a country which had enjoyed peace for half a century. Moreover, in 1561 Philip II made Madrid his permanent capital, and the town slowly began to expand, creating a booming economy of its own. These developments of course had their negative side: the decay of the fairs at Medina del Campo and the shift of the capital from Valladolid moved the centre of activity away from northern Castile, and the great cities there, from Burgos to Toledo, suffered decline and shrank to the level of quiet provincial towns. 'Without the court here, this town is solitary and poor', wrote a Jesuit from Valladolid in 1570.

The predominance of both Seville and Madrid calls for comment. Seville's dual role in the national and the international economy is complex and has not hitherto invited the attentions of any scholar, beyond the multi-volume study of its commerce done by the Chaunus in the 1960s[86]. The city grew in size from about 7,000 households in the 1480s to over 10,000 in 1533 and about 24,000 in the 1590s, remaining steady at this level until the numbers were severely cut by the epidemic of 1649 to about 16,250 households[87]. It functioned chiefly as: an outlet to America of produce from southern Spain; a port of receipt for the bullion and produce of America; a centre for international traders who dealt in these two trades; and an outlet for emigration to the New World. The economic activity of Seville certainly helped to regenerate many sectors of the economy in the mid-sixteenth century, and continued for long thereafter to stimulate sectors such as shipbuilding.

31

But the growing incapacity of Spanish industry to supply America with manufactured goods meant that the gap was quickly filled by foreign traders and their agents resident in Seville, where the foreign colony soon dominated the social and cultural life of the city. Seville's success has therefore been seen as a symbol of the 'dependence' of the Spanish economy on outside producers. From the 1580s, commentators in Castile began to denounce the mechanics of the monopoly system, which effectively worked in favour of foreign finance. Figures for the period show clearly that Seville was no longer really a Spanish port: most of the goods traded out were foreign, and most of that coming in from America went to foreigners[88; 54].

The case of Madrid, studied in detail by Ringrose, offers a parallel example of the negative consequences exercised by a major city over its dependent regions. Whereas a capital like London has been seen by historians as a stimulant to its hinterland, Ringrose sees post-1561 Madrid as a parasite, absorbing population and produce from its surrounding areas but in no real way aiding their growth; the capital 'could provide little stimulus for interior Spain, and may have functioned as a motor for regional economic stagnation'[89]. His thesis is suggestive, and renders the valuable service of looking at the capital within its regional context rather than within the misleading context of the nation; it adds material, moreover, to the debate over 'decline'.

The key role of Madrid and Seville derived in part from their link with international trade. Castile had not been a notable seafaring nation in the later Middle Ages; only the Basques had an active history of seagoing. Catalonia, by contrast, was forced by its environment towards the sea, and thus had a background not only of imperial expansion in the Mediterranean but also of regular trade with Italy. The greater volume of economic power in the peninsula, however, was Castilian, and it is fundamentally the trade of Castile which historians have chosen to study. By the fifteenth century there is ample evidence of the dedication of Castilians to trade with their neighbours, so there can be no foundation for the assumption that Castilians were somehow non-capitalistic. But it is undeniable that Castilian unfamiliarity with the sea meant that much marine trade was transported not by Castilians but by foreigners (English, Dutch, French), who continued throughout the early modern period to dominate the carrying trade, with negative consequences for Spanish economic autonomy. In 1503 the Venetian ambassador, commenting on the influence of Genoese merchants, claimed that 'one third of Genoa is in Spain'. By the seventeenth century the bulk of shipping in Spanish ports was foreign, and there were major commercial centres (such as Alicante) where transport was almost 100 per cent in foreign vessels. Thus analysis of Spanish port statistics (there are studies for Seville, Bilbao, Barcelona) can be deceptive: normally, for instance, an increase in port traffic would suggest an improvement in the regional economy, but in Spain it more likely proves that the economy was being depressed even further by foreign imports. Spanish trade data are hard to find and need to be treated with great caution: an obvious example is the Indies trade operated from Seville and Cadiz, where the official figures are often falsified and misleading.

The important role of American bullion in the economic evolution both of Spain and of Europe was used by Chaunu[86] as a backcloth for his argument that the movements of shipping across the Atlantic coincided with the rise and fall both of prices and of bullion imports. This picture not only confirmed the schema of a 'decline' in Spain in the seventeenth century, it also coincided with the argument of many French historians that the expansion of the sixteenth century ended around 1620, and that a depression set into the European economy from the mid-century. Chaunu's presentation served as the basis for the suggestive chapters on the Atlantic economy in Lynch's work[1]. However, subsequent work by Everaert[88], Kamen [54] and especially Morineau[90], all of them working not on official Spanish returns (which were Hamilton's source) but on the reports of foreign consuls in Seville and Cadiz, has demonstrated that bullion imports from America did not decline during the seventeenth century but rose to unprecedented levels. This conclusion overturns older preconceptions not only on 'decline' but also on the alleged deceleration of the European economy. Little bullion entered the peninsula – it was mostly re-exported both from Spain and from

Europe[45] – but what did may have helped to stabilise prices. Work on the question has helped to fix attention on the major role of the *carrera de Indias* in the evolution of both the peninsular and the world economy.

The economic difficulties of Spain, aggravated by its imperial commitments, have led many historians to consider the entire seventeenth century as a period of profound decay. More recently, it has been argued[12] that the problems, viewed as a structural crisis rather than a 'decline', were concentrated in the last decade of the sixteenth and the first half of the seventeenth century, and that from the 1660s there were signs of renewal in vital sectors; Vilar dates the recovery, specially in the periphery, from the 1680s. The debate has been analysed by Pere Molas[91], but no clear conclusion is possible so long as significant exceptions abound: Domínguez Ortiz affirms, for example, that he can see no recovery in Castile. Given the important variations between regions and sectors, it is obvious that words like 'decline' and 'recovery' have little meaning when applied to the whole country. What then was the situation after the period of crisis? Briefly, in *population* we can say that the north-west (Galicia, Asturias, the Basque country) maintained its levels without interruption, and all the eastern periphery (Catalonia, Valencia, Murcia) showed clear expansion after the 1660s (Casey has cautiously described the evolution of Valencia in the whole century as 'a long depopulation'[62], but the indications from a study of parish records in Guadalest[92], where an annual growth rate of 2.2 per cent could be found after the 1660s, suggest a rapid and remarkable population recovery.) In Old Castile, there was an unmistakable but slow upturn. By contrast, in the whole crescent of south-west Spain (Extremadura, some of New Castile, Andalucia) recovery was hampered by the Portuguese wars and by the epidemics of 1676–85[93]. On balance, and given the exceptions, the rise in the birth rate after 1660 is indisputable; but in perspective the population rise of the late century was little more than a partial recovery of lost ground, so that demographers who consider the whole century to be one of negative growth and decline are also correct.

Despite this equivocal situation, *production* levels per unit

34

farmed rose in most of Spain from the 1660s. It has been suggested, as we have seen[74], that this was because farmers were now, with fewer mouths to feed, cultivating only the better lands. During the same period, there is scattered evidence that livestock levels rose as well. In both demography and output, then, the late seventeenth century was – given the obvious exceptions – a period of hope, whose positive aspects were not confirmed until the next generation. However, the textile industry remained depressed and only a slight rise in output was registered at Segovia: the hopeful sign here was that the government from the 1670s encouraged investment through the Juntas de Comercio[94]. Trade remained firmly in foreign hands, and the decline of Seville during this period was a prelude to the meteoric rise from 1681 of Cadiz, which thereafter became the principal port for American trade. In brief, there was undoubted recovery both in Castile and in the Mediterranean in the vital sectors (population, agriculture and livestock) but in dependent sectors (industry, commerce), more closely related to the European trade pattern, there was little. Thus the economic recuperation of Spain in the seventeenth century was, like its boom in the sixteenth, flawed by basic structural weaknesses.

Despite the continuous participation of Spaniards in trade, industry and agriculture, many historians have argued that Spaniards were anti-capitalist in spirit and in fact. Attempting to explain why Spanish traders were unable to benefit from the favourable conjuncture of the sixteenth century, Braudel[3] proposed the notable thesis of a 'betrayal by the bourgeoisie' (*trahison de la bourgeoisie*), according to which those who were active in trade withdrew their money once they had made their fortunes and thus prejudiced the chance of further capitalist investment. The competence of Spaniards – not only Catalans and Basques but also Castilians – as capitalists during the early modern period has, however, been firmly stressed by several recent writers and most recently by Molas[95], by J. A. Maravall[96] and by Kamen[54]; and there is substantial evidence of Castilians in international trade in the sixteenth century[97]. Two specific problems, those of investment and status, are worth noting here. The presence or absence of a strong native capitalist sector depended obviously on opportunities for investment: we might expect to find the sector in a protected wool market (Burgos) or an average regional port (Barcelona), but the sector might not be strong in a big international port with heavy competition (Seville). The evolution of a capitalist sector, then, was always related to available opportunity and not to any pre-existent 'capitalist spirit'. In the same way, one might invest in government bonds (*juros*) rather than in commerce or agriculture not because one was anti-capitalist but simply because the rate of return was higher: it is significant that at the end of the sixteenth century, when *juros* gave a 7 per cent interest, money flowed into them; but by the late seventeenth, when the rate was down to 5 per cent, money was diverted back into land. The search for status, both then and now, was a normal aspiration for someone who had money but little rank to go with it; and though in some parts of the peninsula those with new status felt that they were required to 'live nobly' there is ample evidence that throughout the early modern period the nouveaux-riches managed to combine both rank and business, so that by the early eighteenth century the trade guilds in the great cities were powerful instruments of the merchant bourgeoisie.

This presentation contradicts the traditional picture, popularised by literary scholars who drew their evidence largely from the imaginative literature of the theatre (Lope de Vega) and the novel (the *Lazarillo*, the *Quijote*), according to which Spaniards were so obsessed by the notion of 'honour' that they were unable to progress economically, thereby dooming their nation to backwardness because of a psychological prejudice. Support has sometimes been given to this view by presenting Spaniards as a nation of (in the words of the contemporary González de Cellorigo) 'bewitched beings, living outside the natural order of things'. Rhetoric apart, there seems to be no justification for thinking that Spaniards, alone of all peoples, lived outside a natural, normal, framework of problems; and the course of Spain's economic history shows few significant divergences from the experience of other nations in Europe.

4 Political Evolution

Between 1450 and 1714 Spain underwent a more extensive political evolution than probably any other west European state of its time. In the late fifteenth century the Spanish realms (one of them Muslim) were a confused collection of jurisdictions with wholly separate identities; by the early eighteenth there remained only one unitary authority, the crown of 'Spain'. Considered thus, the change appears to be striking; but, as elsewhere in old-regime Europe, very much also remained unchanged.

Growth of royal authority was the most important political fact. Given the anarchy of the civil wars in Castile and in Catalonia in the late fifteenth century, there can be little disagreement that the reign of Ferdinand and Isabella initiated the birth of the modern state in Spain. Their obvious success, and the problems of subsequent regimes, helped however to idealise their achievement excessively: 'there can be no monarchy in our Spain, as there was then', wrote Cellorigo in 1600; over three centuries later a conservative pro-Catholic tradition, at its most influential under the Franco regime, went so far as to adopt as its emblem the royal device of Isabella. Traditional Anglo-Saxon historiography, which identified the Spanish rulers as 'new monarchs', drew parallels between them and the dynasties of other emergent nation states such as England and France.

An increase in royal authority did not necessarily imply an increase in state power: one must distinguish between the three realities of *monarquía*, crown and state. The *monarquía*, as we have seen, was simply the union of the various territories under one head; 'all past monarquías began in violence and force of arms', wrote Gregorio López Madera in his *Excellences of the Monarquía of Spain* (1597), 'only that of Spain has had just beginnings, great part of it coming together by succession.'

The crown, or royal power, was more controversial. As early as the fourteenth century the king of Castile had claimed 'absolute power', and in 1439 Juan II stated that 'so great is the king's right to power, that all laws and all rights are subject to him, and his authority is not from men but from God, whose place he occupies in temporal matters'. The claims to 'absolute power' were repeated under the Catholic Kings, and Isabella used the phrase seven times in her testament. Some historians have therefore described the regime of Ferdinand and Isabella as absolutist, and it is even more common to find the regime of Philip II described as such. In effect, pretensions to absolute power can be found only in Castile. Everywhere else in the *monarquía* – Navarre, the Crown of Aragon, Naples, Sicily, the Netherlands – there existed traditional institutions to restrict royal claims, and even in Castile a mediaeval tradition of consultation with the Cortes was affirmed during the Comunidades (1520) and in the 1620s during the opposition to Olivares' regime. In practice, the reality of absolutism can probably be best measured by the success of the crown in *making laws*, whether administrative or fiscal, without the need to obtain consent, or in *by-passing the law*; and by this standard the kings of Spain had considerable power. However, law-making was at best a part-time activity of kings (Philip II made an average of eighteen laws a year, Philip IV about eight); and when we consider the ordinary and daily restrictions on royal authority the concept of absolutism seems to be more of an aspiration than a reality. All legists accepted certain practical limits to absolutism, for instance that the king was still subject to divine law, or that only the king in person could act extra-legally but that he could not oblige the state, itself created by law, to break the law[98].

Though Ferdinand and Isabella initiated nothing new in the constitution, they were singularly successful in getting various interests to respect the law, and their decrees (*pragmáticas*) and those of their successors, suitably codified, became the basis of Castilian legislation. This meant, however, that the Cortes quickly lost its function as a law-making body, despite repeated protests. In a strictly legal sense, then, the crown in Castile (and in America, which depended directly

38

on Castilian law) was sovereign. It was when the crown tried to extend its law-making functions to other parts of the *monarquía* that tensions arose. The king in his non-Castilian realms was bound by the laws of those realms, which used their institutions to try to repel the king. In the peninsula the independent laws of the non-Castilian states were generally known as *fueros*, and every unacceptable action or decree of the king was immediately judged to be an *antifuero* and therefore illegal. A further defence, available in theory also in Castile but more used in America, was the idea that laws be 'obeyed but not put into effect': for example, in 1527 a *fuero* of Vizcaya stated that any royal command 'that is or may be against the laws or fueros, be obeyed but not put into effect'. This usage (*pase foral*) was common in the Basque countries, illustrating the preference for compromise over conflict. Thus the theoretical powers of the crown were cushioned in practice, and it is difficult to single out 'absolute' actions by the crown in early modern Spain. In any case, every sensible monarch liked to be seen to be consulting: Isabella never ceased to maintain that she was absolute, yet took care to pass all her laws inside the Cortes rather than out of it; Charles V granted to the Cortes in 1525 the right to have a permanent standing committee (*Diputación*) along the lines of those existing in the Crown of Aragon; and Philip II, racked by age and gout, nevertheless in 1592 made the long journey to attend the Aragonese Cortes that pacified the realm after the revolt of Antonio Pérez.

Royal power would have been quite hollow had no adminis-trative infrastructure – what I shall call the 'state' – evolved to support it: in a suggestive article of 1960[99], Vicens Vives looked at some problems of the emergent state bureaucracy, and Maravall in subsequent studies[96; 100] showed how the evolution of state theory and administrative mechanisms (e.g. the army) in Spain was closely connected to developments elsewhere in Europe. Bureaucracy was very slow to develop, and down to the early Habsburg period the 'state', as in mediaeval times, consisted of the crown and its immediate officials. Isabella had administered her realm in a mediaeval and astonishingly popular fashion simply by travelling around and taking her officials with her[101], but impressive as this may have been practical requirements soon demanded that more officials be created and that they become sedentary. Institutions and personnel began to develop: law courts (*chancillerías*), councils, secretaries of state[102]. By the reign of Philip II secretaries played a key role in coordinating government, and under Philip V they developed into ministerial heads of department. Of the councils, which derived from late mediaeval models, the most important was the Council of Castile, not only because it oversaw government of the largest of the Spanish realms but also because it was the highest legal body in the *monarquía*; from 1480, the Catholic Kings enforced existing rules about the legal qualifications and training required by its members. The bureaucratic demands of the state stimulated the study of law at university, not only in Spain but in all western countries; at Salamanca and Alcalá canon and civil law swamped other disciplines, matriculations in law at the former during the seventeenth century outnumbering those in theology by twenty to one[103]. The contemporary Diego Hurtado de Mendoza observed that 'the Catholic Kings placed the administration of justice and public affairs into the hands of *letrados*' (law graduates). No innovation in itself, the practice of appointing *letrados* as administrators became generalised: not only the courts and councils were staffed by them, but as many as half the *corregidores* of the sixteenth century were also *letrados*. The lawyers became in effect the new administrative class[104], and since they were almost without exception already of noble (*hidalgo*) rank their rise brought about few status conflicts with the established nobility (unlike France, where prolonged clashes of status took place). Moreover, from the mid-sixteenth century those with doctoral degrees from the principal Castilian and Aragonese universities were granted automatic noble status. It is worth noting that the lawyers were trained either in canon or in civil law or in both, making them eligible for office in both Church and state; Spain was in the probably unique position of having a unitary civil service, with clergy eligible for senior offices of state (many served as viceroys) and laymen eligible for Church posts (some early inquisitors were laymen). Unlike the bureaucracy of the French crown, the *letrado* hierarchy was not venal, that is, their posts were

40

not as a rule bought or sold; this tended to make for greater efficiency and – even more important from the crown's point of view – helped to keep the posts under royal control. Entrenched in the administration, many *letrados* of fairly humble origin went on to found great dynasties of servants of the crown[105]. This by no means meant that the traditional nobility were deprived of their role in government; they still dominated some councils, notably the Council of State, and enjoyed a near-monopoly of the major offices of state (viceroys, ambassadors).

Though bureaucracy began to develop from the end of the fifteenth century, state power did not perceptibly increase. This was because the crown, when building up a body of reliable servants, used them generally not to interfere with or change institutions but to collaborate with them. We can see this in action both in the centre, with ministers of state, and in the provinces, with two key officials, the *corregidor* (or city governor) and the *viceroy*. At the centre the possibility that the office of chief minister, made important by the absence of Charles V and the consequent concentration of authority in the hands of administrators such as Los Cobos[106], might develop into a permanent feature, disappeared with the resolve of Philip II to be his own chief minister. Under this strong king there were several powerful men of state – Antonio Pérez[107], Juan de Idiáquez – but no significant increase in their functions. After Philip's death his weaker successors tended to put more authority in the hands of ministers who were known as *validos*[108], but these too did not implement any institutional change, and the only one with a declared policy, Olivares[25], failed completely to achieve anything. Under the duke of Lerma, though the *valido* made many important decisions, considerable initiative returned to the traditional system of councils[109], and the same process occurred under the *validos* of the time of Charles II. Not until the reign of Philip V did a revolution take place in the conduct of central government.

The corregidors, of late-mediaeval origin, grew to become the crown's key liaison officials in Castile[110], and though there was a brief reaction against them during the Comunidades in 1521, they functioned satisfactorily throughout the

41

Habsburg period, so much so that the new post of *intendant*, introduced in 1711[111], was based explicitly on them. In the non-Castilian realms the crown's chief liaison officer was the viceroy, a post made necessary first by Ferdinand's absence from his realms of Aragon and later by the clear impossibility of any monarch ruling personally in distant realms such as Italy or America. Questions of finance and of law and order inevitably impelled all viceroys to action, thereby bringing royal law into conflict with local privileges. It is clear from the example of Catalonia[112] that viceroys were sometimes able to tamper with the local Cortes, and when acting in conjunction with the king's court of justice, the Audiencia (established in Barcelona in 1493, in Valencia in 1543), the viceroy could issue 'royal' decrees. Though viceroys might win their way over a broad range of issues, they were always aware that the argument must never be forced against local interests, and on balance it is doubtful if royal authority throughout the early modern period was ever permanently extended through its viceroys.

It is thus difficult to see any dramatic advance of state power, a conclusion which necessarily modifies our view of the extent and efficacy of royal authority. The *monarquía* remained firmly decentralised throughout the Habsburg period, with Valladolid acting first as administrative centre and Madrid then being chosen as permanent capital in 1561. This condition of decentralisation was of course common to every other west European state, and was no sign of weakness; indeed, in a federative monarchy such as the Spanish it is possible to view local autonomy as a strength rather than a weakness. We know that vast tracts of the peninsula, including entire cities and regions, were exempt from effective royal control and were under the jurisdiction of the aristocracy and the Church (in Salamanca province the crown exercised jurisdiction over only one-third of the population, in the kingdom of Aragon over probably one-half). How, without any modern civil service, was the government to impose its will in these areas? There was in fact no alternative to attempting a good relationship between crown and regional autonomies, which explains the respect in which the crown held both the local nobility and the municipal oligarchies.

Thompson has described[15] how the pressure of finance and war obliged Philip II to set up central bodies to take care of taxes, recruitment and supplies; but he also shows how in the later years of the reign the crown gave up on centralised control, contracted out for supplies and put *more* authority into the hands of its regional nobility, who alone could organise local defences. In the great cities, in effect, government was almost wholly autonomous, with tenuous royal control being maintained through the corregidor (who existed anyway only in the largest towns) and through the royal courts; local administration, however, has not received the attention it deserves[113].

In only one area did the crown make a determined effort to impose its will: finance. Ferdinand and Isabella began the policy of debt[114] and created both personnel and mechanisms (such as *juros*) to deal with it; under Charles V a more sophisticated system prepared Castile for its long career of imperial finance[14]. The Council of Finance which evolved from 1523 was responsible in fact for the financing not only of Castile but of all royal enterprises throughout the *monarquía*, making it unique among the administrative bodies. The alarming increase in government debt has been extensively studied[17] and the impact of fiscality on Castile is well known[115]; taxes rose steadily throughout the sixteenth and early seventeenth centuries, declining only in the later seventeenth. Though it might seem that by stepping up taxation the state was increasing its authority, precisely the reverse happened in Spain, where the crown was obliged to take the highly negative step of giving up areas of its jurisdiction. This occurred in two main ways: real tax income was assigned away to creditors in order to repay long-term debts (*juros*), and important areas of patronage were alienated in order to obtain ready cash. The granting of tax income as *juros* was so extensive that by the end of the sixteenth century the crown had mortgaged virtually all its regular income, and relied heavily on the special grants or *servicios* made by the Cortes. The sale of offices in Castile, known in the fifteenth century and attempted by Charles V in the 1520s, began on a large scale in the 1540s and involved the widespread alienation of municipal posts formerly in crown patronage:

between 1543 and 1584 over 2,928 posts of *regidor* (city councillor) were sold[116]. In the early seventeenth century[117] the crown also sold townships (the so-called 'sale of vassals'). It is difficult not to conclude that the consequence of such alienations was an effective decrease in crown authority.

The traditional view of the Cortes of Castile during the Habsburg period is that it was 'little more than a rubber stamp', with royal authority supreme in the decadent seventeenth century. The considerable increase in *servicios*, however, which rose from being about a quarter of royal income in the 1570s to over half in the early seventeenth century, meant that ironically the crown began to depend heavily on the Cortes, which took the opportunity to criticise the long, expensive war in the Netherlands, and to demand that conditions be set for the granting of the *servicios*. In the closing years of Philip II and during the reign of his son, there was an impressive outbreak of constitutionalism in Castile, with members of the Cortes openly proclaiming contractual and democratic principles; Cortes sessions also became more regular, rising to an average of eight months a year as compared to less than two months a year in the mid-sixteenth century[118]. Government ministers bullied and bribed, but from 1600 were forced to accept a contractual agreement that if taxes were voted grievances must be redressed. Thus in Castile, as elsewhere in western Europe, there were successful moves to put taxation on a constitutional basis; and though the Cortes were never summoned during the late seventeenth century the government continued to consult directly with the municipalities normally represented there. The constitutional initiative of the Cortes should of course be set in context: it was a short-term achievement, the taxes themselves were usually granted, and no political advantages were gained; but the whole matter is clear testimony to an active political consciousness among the ruling elite of the cities of Castile.

We must remember above all that the innovative 'state' was still only a small part of government. Pre-industrial Europe was largely self-governing, with highly localised structures, a simple fact which explains for example the ability of Spain to rule itself through the long years of Charles V's absences.

What were these traditional structures? At the upper level, each realm had its own assembly, ranging from territories with formalised Cortes (Castile, Crown of Aragon[119], Navarre[120]) to those with elective bodies (the Junta General of Vizcaya[121]). The crown's representative had the right to be present at these meetings, as he was also entitled to be present at all formal assemblies of the Church; but it was rare for the crown to interfere in the process of decision-making. The elite was also left largely undisturbed in control of the government of the great cities, a control made even more secure by the crown's practice – at its most extensive under Philip II – of selling municipal office in order to raise cash, both in Spain and in America. Thus government in Spain throughout the Habsburg period was typically regional and autonomous, rather than national. This did not weaken the crown; on the contrary, it minimised the need for the crown to create a broad and expensive bureaucracy, and it also helped to fragment local opposition whenever it arose (for example, when Saragossa threatened to revolt against Philip II in 1591, not a single other city risked sending military help to the rebels).

At the lower level, traditional structures were based on community authority. Many villages and towns continued the medieval practice of self-government based on the *concejo abierto* (village council), but by the sixteenth century much of this was a memory and communalism was more to be found in economic structures, mainly agriculture, than in political life. A broader community solidarity continued however to exist in defined cultural areas which shared common customs, language and domestic economy. Much of the reality of political life in pre-industrial Spain was based at this local level, from which external authority (whether of king or lord or Church) was brusquely excluded, and within which both loyalties and conflicts, often kin-based, were frequently contained[122]. In many major cities, authority from generation to generation was jealously divided between groups of families and any attempt to upset the equilibrium provoked violence[123].

In Habsburg Spain the crown always took care to have mechanisms of consultation, even if Cortes were not called, and the writings of the *arbitristas* are evidence of the considerable freedom of public discussion to be found in the country[124]. It has been too frequently assumed that there was no liberty to differ or to speak out, an assumption based no doubt on the existence of an Inquisition; but it remains to be demonstrated whether any thought-control existed or could have existed; and by contrast there is ample evidence of the preference of Spaniards for freedom, expressed openly in writings which never hesitated to criticise injustice and especially in a rich tradition of political thought, notably represented by the Jesuit thinkers of the late sixteenth century[125]. The absolutist theories of a writer like Juan Fernández Medrano, who claimed that 'subjects are obliged to obey princes even when these order something against the interests of the people and against civil justice' (1602), may be balanced by the democratism of the Jesuit Juan de Mariana or by the claim of a member of the Cortes in 1621 that 'the king has no absolute power', or by the opinion of Diego Pérez de Mesa, asserting in the same decade that 'all subjects are naturally free and fundamentally equal'[126]. Spanish thinkers were heavily influenced by foreign, especially Italian, theorists, and though some of their writings have an old-fashioned air there were also many who were not only aware of the main issues of their day but also made pioneering and positive contributions to political thinking. There is little reason to treat Spain as a case apart, as though it were a tyranny or an oriental despotism (significantly, the attacks of Mariana and Suárez against tyranny, written around 1600, were condemned in Paris and in London but never in Madrid): in its broad lines of evolution, as Maravall has convincingly shown[96], Spain was fully a part of the western tradition. Effective political protest was inevitably limited to the elites who controlled the great cities: their finest hour appears to have been in the early 1600s, when the Cortes representative for Granada led the opposition to Olivares[127].

Spain was no more exempt than other countries from the threat of popular revolt; like other Europeans, Spaniards were ready to rise against oppression, whether state, seigneurial or ecclesiastical. In 1520 the great turmoil of the Comunidades[128] – which included substantial popular

46

agitation[129] – initiated the large-scale movements of the early modern period. Thereafter we know of no major risings until the Granada revolts of the Moriscos in 1569, but in the meantime many dissatisfied Moriscos contributed hugely to public disorder by their participation in banditry in the eastern half of the peninsula[130]. After the Morisco expulsions of 1609–14, however, it was the turn of the Christian population, both in the south and in Valencia, to take on the role of the depressed and exploited; moreover, the crisis conditions of the early century provoked discontent. The only revolts to have been studied in detail so far are the 1640 crisis in Catalonia[38], the crisis of 1648–52 in Andalucia[131], and the uprisings of 1688 and 1693 on the Mediterranean coast[132]. These movements usually provoked armed repression, because of their size. More typical of popular revolt, however, are the local incidents – such as the 1631 riots in Vizcaya – that have never found their historian and which therefore go by default. Given the variety of jurisdictions within Spain, many revolts (as in Valencia in 1693 and again during the War of Succession) were directed neither against the state nor against fiscality but against the seigneurial regime, so that once again the role of the state was often minimal.

Like other European nations in the mid-seventeenth century, Spain faced a crisis of government based on fiscality. Thanks, however, to the great extension of the *monarquía*, the Spanish problem was also one of tension between regional autonomy and central authority. Interpretations of the period of crisis, stretching from the events in Aragon in 1591 to the Portuguese and Catalan revolts of 1640, the Naples revolt of 1647–8 and the Palermo rebellion of 1674, are useful yet still require further analysis. Within the peninsula, for example, use of the word 'revolt' can be highly misleading. It is impossible to talk of 'the revolt of Aragon' in 1591 (there was no such revolt, troubles being restricted to Saragossa). The so-called 'revolt of the Catalans' was far more complex than either the notion of 'revolt' or the old image of 'Catalonia vs Castile' might imply. Elliott shows clearly[38] that in 1640 much of the wrath in the principality was in fact directed by ordinary Catalans against their own ruling classes, and few favoured the alliance with France; Sanabre's classic study[38]

47

documents convincingly the opposition of the population to the French. In the post-1653 period, after the recovery of Barcelona, the elites inevitably played down their part in events, but there is growing evidence that the rebels were never more than a small faction. Recently Vidal Pla has looked at the evolution of the royalist party in the province and shows how, while 'the higher nobility abandoned at once the political programme of Pau Claris' and the duchess of Cardona organised pro-royalist resistance from her estates, after 1643 there was widespread defection to the cause of Philip IV: 'the Generalitat, representing the political revolution, and the peasant farmers, representing the popular revolution, had a coincidence of interests in July 1640; but the unity did not last and contradictions between nobles and peasant farmers opened up, leading to popular uprisings throughout the war years'[133]. This picture helps to shift the focus from the old image of a deep-rooted and permanent conflict between Castile on one hand and Catalonia on the other. The reconciliation of the two in the late seventeenth century has been firmly demonstrated[134], making it difficult to accept the view that Catalonia once again 'revolted' during the War of Succession; and apart from clear evidence that the commercial elite of Barcelona and Mataró supported the archduke between 1705 and 1714 with the intention of gaining trade advantages[135], there is little or no evidence of any widespread rebellion in Catalonia, current research tending to show that Catalans were neutral and merely supported whichever side happened to be dominant at the time[136]. This brings the picture into line with what we know of the other realms of the Crown of Aragon, where one finds a similar lack of evidence for rebellion: there were notable defections to the Allied cause, but the overwhelming bulk of the elite and of the towns remained solidly faithful to Philip V, declaring for the pretender only when military occupation gave them no other alternative[20]. The administrative changes brought about by the new Bourbon monarchy during the War of Succession were of capital importance and represent the first major step taken since the epoch of the Catholic Monarchs towards the creation of a united Spain. For the first time, a real programme of centralisation was carried out, taxes were reformed, constitutional privileges (in Aragon) were abolished, a national army and navy were created. These changes were wholly revolutionary, but look forward to an epoch which is beyond the confines set by the present essay[137]: after Utrecht Spain no longer had a European empire, and could devote itself to a century of recuperation and resurgence.

5 Society and Culture

The coexistence of three major religions – Islam, Christianity and Judaism – in the peninsula for some seven centuries, had a formative influence on the character of Spain and has coloured its historiography. The interpretations have frequently merged with both ideology and nationalism: for many scholars, both Spanish and foreign, Spain is 'different' to an extent that requires special categories and a special type of explanation. Américo Castro has been among the most influential proponents of such a view in this century[7]. Taken together with some older opinions about Spain (their alleged non-capitalist mentality, for example), these theories present Spaniards as a nation with attitudes distinct from those found in the rest of Europe. More recent scholars (notably J. A. Maravall) have insisted by contrast that Spain was not as isolated from the western tradition as has been believed.

The theory of isolation relies firstly on the multicultural experience of Spain down to the end of the Reconquest era, and then on the apparent separation of Spain from European currents from the reign of Philip II onwards. Because Spain seemed to have a separate development in both mediaeval and modern times, some scholars have maintained that Spain had no Renaissance, no Baroque and no Counter Reformation. The notion of 'difference', however, goes further. Certain social characteristics – extreme religious zeal, exaggerated concepts of honour, a perverse pride in poverty – were and are viewed as being peculiarly Spanish and rooted in the history of Spaniards. Both socially and culturally the nation has been thought of as a world apart. This isolationist view can be found among scholars of all persuasions: it has appealed to traditionalists because it emphasises 'Spanish' values; it has appealed to non-Spaniards, because it confirms the romantic image of a nation living in the past; and it has been

51

sustained by 'liberal' Spaniards, who have used it to condemn the backwardness of their country.

Greater use by scholars of comparative disciplines such as sociology and social anthropology[138], has more recently made it obvious that despite certain inevitable differences the experience of Spaniards was not unique. In the evolution both of class and of culture, the same forces common to western Europe could be shown to have been active in the peninsula. A Castilian mercantile and bourgeois class was active in western Europe both before and after the discovery of America[139], working closely with other trading interests, notably with the Genoese and their Mediterranean trade[140]. Mercantile fortunes were made, and the early capitalist spirit was as active as anywhere else. Though many writers continued to sneer at wealth and to praise mediaeval warrior values, a moneyed bourgeoisie, fattened by trade, developed in Spain[95]. The problem, in Spain as in other western countries, is to trace the evolution of this bourgeoisie, which covered its tracks because its only social aspiration was to attain noble rank and because the vicissitudes of trade caused many fortunes to dwindle. Moreover, whereas the 'bourgeoisie' can normally be identified with the urban middle classes, in the Mediterranean this middle class tended to take the form of a patriciate with noble status, so that in practice it was difficult to distinguish between bourgeois and noble. The 'dependent' status of Spain's commercial relations, above all, left few opportunities open to the native bourgeois, and – as in parts of eastern Europe – some nobles were using their resources to enter the market. The clearly secondary role of the Spanish bourgeoisie did not prevent them being strong and influential at a local level, especially in the seaports, as with the elite of *ciutadans honrats*[141] in Catalonia and similar groups in Valencia, but their wider commercial links were very fragile, and in late-seventeenth-century Valencia for example only the merchants of foreign origin appear to have had good international contacts. Problems of honour and status were less deep-rooted than is often imagined: sixteenth-century writers admitted freely that 'large-scale trading' was as honourable a profession as arms or letters, and in 1622 one of the Military Orders opened its ranks to 'merchants'.

Controversy over the status of commerce continued well into the eighteenth century[142], as in England and in France, but long before then there was no practical barrier to the social ascent of those who had made fortunes in large-scale or sea-going trade; the prejudice was restricted to small-scale trade and shopkeeping. A shift of attitudes did not by itself facilitate the development of a bourgeoisie; that came only during the eighteenth century, with the growth of the economy and the breakdown of the systems of foreign monopoly control. Some historians have attributed Spain's economic problems to the absence of a capitalistic ethic and the consequent lack of an effective bourgeoisie; this is arguably to put the cart before the horse, and it appears more justifiable to maintain that Spain, like other western nations, had both a bourgeoisie and an ethic, but that the negative economic situation prejudiced both. Even when further work is done on the problem, the debate will go on.

The negative vision of Spain's bourgeoisie has been exceeded only by the negative vision of its aristocracy, commonly presented as backward and anti-capitalist. It is obvious that the aristocracy encapsulated traditional values, with an emphasis on the warrior ethic and the primacy of agriculture over trade. Under Ferdinand and Isabella all known accessions to the rank of noble were based on distinction in warfare[143]. But, as in other countries, the recruitment of the noble class into the governing bureaucracy helped to confuse the noble ethic, and under Philip II writers complained that the pen had now replaced the sword and that the Castilian aristocracy had forgotten how to fight, thanks to the long peace under Charles V. Moreover, the entry of new-rich merchants and others into the noble class created a war of ideas, with the older aristocracy insisting that only blood descent was valid while the newcomers argued, consonant with Renaissance ideals, that service to the state, whether in the bureaucracy or in the universities or in warfare, bestowed a more valid title to noble status[144]. Spain – like England and France – continued to be run by its noble elite, but this elite continued constantly to renew itself, and the humble but noble bureaucratic families of an earlier epoch evolved into great dynasties. In a country with such an ample range of noble status, from the humble hidalgo to the great grandee, problems of rank and precedence continued to have extraordinary importance, and most of the great professional corporations that evolved in the early modern period laid down rules that excluded people who were not of 'noble' origin (the criterion often adopted was anti-semitic, that is, one had to be free – *limpio* – of Jewish origins). The trend towards aristocratisation thus intensified, as in France and England, with constant social mobility leading to a proliferation in the number of noble titles granted by the state. This 'inflation of honours', though provoked in part by the wish of the crown to raise cash through sales[145], was also a real reflection of the upward progress of the moneyed and landed elite, proving that Spanish society was not fixed into immovable status categories.

Although several studies have been done on the evolution of noble fortunes, little is known of the public role of the great families[146]. The impressive extent of noble control over the land is now well documented for much of Spain[147], but though there are obviously negative aspects of any social system where wealth is in only a few hands, it is unclear whether this was exclusively harmful. Certainly the naïve image of all nobles as being doomed by their ethic to do no work, must be rejected. Though grandees were necessarily absent from their estates, these were usually carefully managed, were protected from fragmentation by the system of *mayorazgo*, and figured among the country's leading sources of grain and wool, so that their economic role cannot be underestimated[77; 54]. Participation of Spanish nobles in industry and trade was logical, commonplace and did not detract from their status. Survival of the documentation of noble houses has demonstrated the fairly efficient functioning of the great aristocratic estates and their struggle for solvency during the crisis years of the early modern period[148]. By the more tranquil years of the later century, many nobles were triumphing over the crisis; we have the case in Cuidad Real of a knight of Calatrava, Don Gonzalo Muñoz Treviño (1609–70), who accumulated property and land, with an impressive output of wool, grain and wine, and whose neighbours commented on his capitalist mentality: 'he was never seen or known to spend excessively except when it benefited his holdings'[149].

At the other end of the social scale, the only progress made towards a study of the mass of the population has been through the modes of survival: birth, death, diet, poverty. The evidence suggests that in Spain standards of living deteriorated in modern times, with the documentation speaking more of emigration and misery than of betterment. Between about 1530 and 1560 the proportion of registered poor in the cities of Castile increased from about 10 per cent of the population to an average of 23 per cent[50]; the figures do not include unregistered poor such as vagabonds. From the 1580s (as in much of western Europe) mass poverty increased and abandoned infants became a serious problem; an explosion of beggars provoked repressive legislation and there were recommendations, from writers such as Cristóbal Pérez de Herrera, for the adoption of a positive policy. Spanish writers of the time tend to give the impression that most beggars in the peninsula were the dregs of other nations; in fact, Spain had its own problems, as the censuses of 1561 and 1597 bear out (the latter census states, for example, that in the town of Arévalo 56 per cent were registered poor), and in Spain, unlike some other countries, widespread poverty was doomed to become a structural characteristic of its underdevelopment. The recent study of Palencia by Marcos Martín gives a solid guide to the lot of Spaniards in one region[150]; other studies have concentrated on the operation of poor relief[151]. There were and are varying opinions over the causes of the poverty: the most frequently cited reason – heavy taxation – may have affected the truly poor less than is thought, since they were exempt, and it may be more convincing to look at larger structural factors such as changes in land use and the collapse of rural investment[77]. It is possible, in any case, that *inequitable distribution* rather than the weight of taxation was what had the most negative effects, and it may be doubted whether Spaniards were any more heavily taxed than other nations.

Picaresque literature[152], however, tended after 1600 to disseminate the image of a Spain steeped in poverty, and foreign travellers helped to perpetuate the picture of a nation of idle nobles and ragged peasants[153]. Political factors, together with the Inquisition, may have helped to increase incomprehension of the situation in the peninsula; whatever the reason, Dr Johnson was no doubt right to comment of Spain that there was 'no country less known to the rest of Europe'. Not much is known, to be sure, of the interchange of cultural images between the peninsula and the outside world. It is commonly assumed that when Philip II returned to Spain in 1559 he sealed the country off from foreign influences; in practice, such an objective could never have been fully achieved, given that during the age of empire Spaniards were the most travelled nation in the world, including in their orbit not only the whole of Europe but also the New World and Asia. Moreover, there is no sign whatever of any restriction on personal and commercial links with Italy (nearly half of which was within the Spanish *monarquía*)[154]; and links with the Netherlands though sometimes restricted were never cut. These two nations continued to enjoy a lasting and profound relationship with the Iberian peninsula, as we can see by their close commercial, financial, artistic and intellectual links[155]. Just as the military capacity of Spain was enhanced by its confederates within the *monarquía*, so the cultural creativity of the Golden Age drew on much foreign inspiration and was not exclusively Hispanic: the deep debt to Italy of Spanish art, poetry and music is too well known to need comment. These close international links nevertheless remained ambivalent: Italians, for example, had good political reasons for distrusting Spain, and the comments of both their ambassadors and their distinguished visitors (both nobles and prelates) were uniformly hostile. The relative isolation of Spain, then, seems to owe less to the existence of censorship than to political tensions: a typical case is that of relations with France. Spaniards read and admired Bodin and Montaigne in translation, published their own books freely in French territory (in the late sixteenth and early seventeenth century over one hundred Spanish authors had their works printed in Lyon, without any criticism from the Spanish authorities), and those who could read the language purchased French books avidly[156]; none of this ever dispelled the element of distrust.

The active cultural links of Spain need emphasising, in view of the still prevailing impression that the peninsula was in some way culturally strangled. Technical backwardness was in fact one of the reasons why publishing never became big business in the peninsula: without any sophisticated printing presses of its own, Spain was obliged to resort to the printers of Antwerp and of Lyon, and thanks to this managed to maintain an effective literary output throughout the early modern period[157]. Censorship indubitably had a restricting effect[158], as it had in every European country, but it is worth remarking that the prohibitions of the famous inquisitorial Indices of the sixteenth century applied overwhelmingly to foreign-language books which had never been within the reach of Spaniards anyway[159].

The spiritual and Church history of the Golden Age is heavily affected by the absence of any Reformation in Spain. The failure of heresy to penetrate the peninsula remains a puzzle: the Church was as backward and corrupt there as anywhere else (no reforms were carried out by the Catholic Monarchs, apart from some reorganisation of the main religious orders, so that the old image of a purified Church can be safely rejected), and though the Inquisition was vigilant it could not hope to censor every one of the hundreds of books that entered Spain every year (between 1557 and 1564 one merchant alone, Andrés Ruiz, imported 1,012 bales of books from France; we can only conjecture the full total of volumes imported annually). One may also reject the picture of a solidly Catholic nation that refused to countenance error, since Spain appears, like other countries, to have had its share of unbelievers and half-believers. The most likely brief explanation is that the multi-cultural background concentrated attention so much on confrontation with Judaism and Islam that it allowed little scope, then as in the mediaeval epoch, to dissent within the Christian body; and the absence of heresy thus offered no basis on which heterodoxy could build in the way that Reformation thought in England could build on Lollardy. When dissent did arise in the sixteenth century, it was among those who were heirs to the multi-cultural background: the *conversos*. Thus from several perspectives the emergence of the mystical *alumbrados* can be seen as

57

a crucial event[160]. A product of the new spirituality, but also probably influenced by their semitic background, the *alumbrados* prepared the way for the neo-Protestant groups that sprang up in Castile and Andalucia; their postulates appealed to an elite culture that also embraced the doctrines of Erasmus with enthusiasm[161]. Erasmianism itself, though popular among many intellectuals, was essentially a 'court' movement, and its high-tide (1520–30) coincided almost exactly with Charles V's first sojourn in Spain. The open-mindedness of Spaniards at this period was based less on humanism than on a consciousness of plurality of interests; it was the epoch of the Lutheran Reformation, but many were willing to approach that phenomenon with a caution bordering on tolerance, rather than with repression[162]. Only the discovery of Protestant cells in Spain in 1558 shocked them out of their complacency[163].

This brings us to the significance of the Inquisition[164]. In the Black Legend and in the 'decline' myth, a major part of the blame for Spain's ills was borne by the Inquisition. Study of the tribunal has in recent years become a growth industry, and ideological heat has fortunately been removed from the debate, allowing us to see the Holy Office not as an organ of totalitarian control but as a judicial body which had an enormous impact in the repressive period of its existence (1480–1520), when it executed the greatest number of people (virtually all of Jewish descent) ever put to death till then by a European state for ideological reasons, but which thereafter played an auxiliary rather than a dominant role. Intensive archive research has produced interesting statistical details[165] and valuable perspectives on the tribunal in its day-to-day work; but the very volume of such research may help to exaggerate its role, and studies which are now in preparation[166] suggest that attention should also be focussed on other related mechanisms in religio-cultural life. The importance of the Inquisition cannot be doubted: it was a repressive body which terrorised the cultural minorities[167], and had a highly negative influence on intellectual freedom; but there is no evidence whatever to show that by itself it hurt literature[159], the arts or the sciences, or that it isolated Spain from Europe. Moreover, given the small number of its personnel, it seems likely – a conclusion which remains controversial – that its real impact on the daily lives of most Spaniards between 1520 and 1834 (when it was finally abolished) was very marginal. The gap between what it professed and what it actually put into practice was always considerable: from the late sixteenth century its censorship of books was erratic and often only symbolic, and its operation of the anti-semitic *limpieza de sangre* regulations was at best reluctant, leading by the 1580s to a well-mounted campaign by the Inquisition itself to modify and abolish them[168].

Historians to date have concentrated on the exclusively ecclesiastical aspects of the Church in Spain, such as participation in Trent and the reform of the religious orders. Approaching the subject from this angle has tended to confirm the traditional image of a solidly Catholic country where nothing changed over the centuries. New perspectives opened up by French and Italian studies, however, have shown the importance of attention to the real state of religious belief and practice, as seen through such sources as pastoral visits made to dioceses by the bishops[169]. Since religion played such a fundamental part at all stages of life, from the cradle to the grave, the impact of the Counter Reformation on social rites such as popular feasts (*fiestas*) and other activities of man in his communal context, have also been examined. William Christian has continued the enquiry into communal religion by looking at attitudes to local saints and to apparitions of the Virgin[170]. The Inquisition took an interest in these questions, and its role in the problem of witchcraft, placed long ago in perspective by Henry Charles Lea[164], has been further examined recently[171]. The interesting aspect is that whereas in most other countries witches during this period were executed, the Spanish clergy (like those of Italy) refused to treat the phenomenon as heresy, so that clear directives from the Inquisition in 1526 and in 1610 made sure that witch-burning was virtually unknown. This conclusion, however, is only partially valid, since in practice the secular authorities, whose records remain to be studied, continued to execute witches by hanging.

These forays into popular religion have usefully opened up the debate over how Catholic Spain really was. The traditional picture, presented brilliantly by the exegete Menéndez y Pelayo in several writings[172], was of a solidly Catholic country which stoutly resisted the Reformation and rightly ousted the Jews and Moriscos. What we know of religious practice and belief, especially in the rural and mountainous regions of Spain, shows on the contrary that Catholicism and Catholic morality was often little more than a veneer on popular practices: an interesting example is the prevalence of the opinion, actively castigated by the Inquisition during the period of the Counter Reformation, that sexual intercourse ('fornication') between unmarried adults was not sinful[173]. It is also apparent that religious hostility to the cultural minorities was not always as profound as official propaganda pretended, and that a practical tolerance could be found not only at elite level but also among sections of the population[162]. This complex picture inevitably has much to do with regional differences within Spain (anti-semitism was rare in Catalonia, for example, in part because of the tiny Jewish population), and confirms the conclusion that it would be misleading to write of the culture and literature of the Golden Age only in terms of 'the Castilian mind'[174]. Recent study of the contact-point between elite and popular cultures, particularly in the theatre and in public leisure activities, has added a new dimension to literary studies and helped to rescue the subject from being a mere study of texts by Castilian authors[175]. The social study of religion, in brief, illuminates the surprising richness of attitudes that underlay the official postulates of belief during the Golden Age.

6 Conclusion

The very uniqueness of Spain's historical experience – the centuries of coexistence with Islam and Judaism, the fortunate discovery of a stupendous New World, the sudden inheritance of universal empire – might mislead us into searching for a unique explanation of its subsequent evolution. Like Don Quixote in his search for the fabulous, scholars have often looked for the unique ingredient that makes Spain different, and in the process have created an image woven out of the dreams of Spaniards themselves. 'When in ancient or modern times', exclaimed a sixteenth-century conquistador of Peru, Francisco de Jérez, 'have there been such great enterprises of so few against so many, through so many lofty climates and vast seas and endless lands, to conquer the unseen and unknown? Who can equal those of Spain?' The meteoric rise to world status of 'those of Spain' – 'los de España' – has seemed almost inexplicable, and the subsequent collapse even more inexplicable. Out of this dramatic vision of history was born the concept of 'decline', which Spaniards themselves fostered in the nineteenth century when they came to criticise the failures of their own country[12], and which was seized upon and used by non-Spanish historians. There is certainly evidence that (as later in 1898) the failures of the epoch produced much introspective pessimism[57], but pessimism cannot always be taken as a reflection of reality, and indeed produced at the time its own myths, such as the belief that Spain had been powerful and prosperous under Ferdinand and Isabella, and declined only after them. Pessimism, moreover, had its own special heyday, during the depression of the early seventeenth century, whereas a slightly longer perspective shows that outside that period the imagery of ruin was fading[54]. The concept of 'decline', in effect, is no longer used by working historians, as a guide to what really happened in early modern Spain.

Recent research leaves us, by contrast, with the unsurprising image of a poor country that was given every opportunity to benefit from leadership of an empire it had never had to conquer, but which lost that opportunity: it is the how and why of this problem that continues to attract controversy. The will to succeed is probably not in doubt: Castilians proved to be superb soldiers, good administrators, adequate traders; and if they fell behind in any of these spheres they received solid support from Italians, Flemings and the other peoples of the *monarquía*. Nonetheless, almost from the beginning there were clear signs that Spain's experience was not going to duplicate the achievements of the Roman Empire. Although leader of a world monarchy, Spain relied overwhelmingly on foreign money, foreign troops and foreign ships to sustain that leadership, an inverted situation to be found in no other empire in history; coloniser of the American continent, it almost from the first ceased to be able to control the political and economic destiny of the New World; commercial crossroads of the west, it failed to reap the benefits of that trade and became a colony for European merchants; recipient of the gold and silver of the Indies, its population began to experience, and for generations, the pangs of poverty. Inevitably, seventeenth-century writers came to judge the whole imperial experience as a tragic mistake, and we can see with hindsight that the Golden Age, if it existed, was there for the few but not for the many. Even the application of the term 'golden' to culture may raise doubts: imperialism promoted the Castilian language and Castilian culture, but at the cost of the Arabic, Catalan and other traditions of the peninsula; moreover, the impact on Europe was fleeting, and it is significant that the image it most successfully projected on to the rest of the world in the early seventeenth century was an ambivalent one, the delusions of a Don Quixote, the vagabond escapism of a Guzmán de Alfarache.

Was the Golden Age therefore an illusion? The answer to that question depends on one's political and moral views (many nineteenth-century Spaniards condemned the entire period as one of tyranny, bigotry and racism), on one's personal consciousness of Spain (much Catalan historiography, for example, plays down the positive aspects of Castile's role), and on the perspective one takes of history.

Select Bibliography

Introduction

[1] John Lynch, *Spain under the Habsburgs*, 2nd edn, 2 vols (Oxford, 1981). For the earlier period including the reign of the Catholic Kings, see also J. N. Hillgarth, *The Spanish Kingdoms, 1250–1516* 2 vols (Oxford, 1978), vol. 2.

[2] Jaume Vicens Vives, *Approaches to the History of Spain* (University of California, 1969) (first Spanish edn, 1952), was a pioneering essay of interpretation.

[3] Fernand Braudel, *The Mediterranean and the Mediterranean World in the Age of Philip II*, 2 vols (London, 1972–3).

[4] Pierre Vilar, *La Catalogne dans l'Espagne moderne. Recherches sur les fondements économiques des structures nationales*, 3 vols (Paris, 1962). His brief *Histoire de l'Espagne* (Paris, 1958), achieved wide circulation in Spain. For an assessment of his influence on Spanish scholarship, see Roberto Fernández (ed.), *España en el siglo XVIII. Homenaje a Pierre Vilar* (Barcelona, 1985), with contributions from fifteen historians.

[5] Louis Henry, *Manuel de démographie historique* (Paris–Geneva, 1967).

[6] *Historia de Asturias*, 1977–; *Historia de Andalucia*, in which the most relevant volume is vol. IV, *La Andalucia del Renacimiento (1504–1621)* (Madrid, 1980); for Granada, see *Historia de Granada*, vol. III, *La Epoca Moderna* (Granada, 1986).

[7] Américo Castro, *The Structure of Spanish History* (Princeton, 1954).

[8] Pierre Chaunu, *Histoire et Décadence* (Paris, 1981), a general essay with only passing reference to Spain.

[9] Pedro Saínz Rodríguez, *La evolución de las ideas sobre la decadencia española* (Madrid, 1962), with a useful bibliography.

[10] Earl J. Hamilton, 'The Decline of Spain', *Economic History Review*, VIII (1937–8) 168–79; repr. in E. M. Carus-Wilson (ed.), *Essays in Economic History*, 3 vols (London, 1954–62), I, 215–26.

[11] John H. Elliott, 'The Decline of Spain', *Past and Present*, 20 (Nov. 1961), repr. in T. H. Aston (ed.), *Crisis in Europe, 1560–1660* (London, 1965).

[12] Henry Kamen, 'The Decline of Spain: a historical myth?', *Past and Present*, 81 (Nov. 1978).

Spain as a Great Power

[13] Sverker Arnoldsson, *La Leyenda Negra: estudios sobre sus orígenes* (Göteborg, 1960); W. S. Maltby, *The Black Legend in England* (Durham, N.C., 1971).

[14] Ramón Carande, *Carlos V y sus banqueros: I. La vida económica de Castilla* (Madrid, 1943); *II. La Hacienda Real de Castilla* (Madrid, 1949); *III. Los caminos del oro y de la plata* (Madrid, 1967).

[15] I. A. A. Thompson, *War and Government in Habsburg Spain, 1560–1620* (London, 1976).

[16] René Quatrefages, 'Etat et armée en Espagne au début des temps modernes', *Mélanges de la Casa de Velázquez*, xvii (1981) 85–103. A useful Spanish survey of modern (mainly English) work is L. A. Ribot García, 'El ejercito de los Austrias. Aportaciones recientes y nuevas perspectivas', *Pedralbes*, 3 (1983) 89–126.

[17] Felipe Ruiz Martín, 'Gastos ocasionados por . . . la guerra: repercusiones en España', in V. Barbagli Bagnoli (ed.), *Domanda e Consumi. Livelli e strutture (secoli XIII–XVIII)* (Florence, 1978). On finances, Modesto Ulloa, *La Hacienda Real de Castilla en el reinado de Felipe II*, 2nd edn (Madrid, 1977); F. Ruiz Martín, 'Las finanzas españolas durante el reinado de Felipe II', *Cuadernos de Historia, anexos de la revista 'Hispania'*, 2 (1968); also his 'La banca en España hasta 1782', in *El Banco de España. Una historia económica* (Madrid, 1970); Antonio Domínguez Ortiz, *Política y Hacienda de Felipe IV* (Madrid, 1960).

[18] R. A. Stradling, *Europe and the Decline of Spain: a study of the Spanish System, 1580–1720* (London, 1981). This also has a useful bibliography, mainly in English.

[19] Geoffrey Parker, *The Army of Flanders and the Spanish Road, 1567–1659* (Cambridge, 1972); *Spain and the Netherlands* (London, 1979). Aspects of the navy are discussed in J. F. Guilmartin, *Gunpowder and Galleys. Changing technology and Mediterranean warfare at sea in the sixteenth century* (Cambridge, 1974).

[20] Henry Kamen, *The War of Succession in Spain 1700–1715* (London, 1969).

[21] José Alcalá Zamora, *Historia de una empresa siderúrgica española: los altos hornos de Liérganes y La Cavada, 1622–1834* (Santander, 1974); a general survey in V. Vázquez de Prada, 'La industria siderúrgica en España (1500–1650)', in H. Kellenbenz (ed.), *Schwerpunkte der Eisengewinnung und Eisenverarbeitung in Europa, 1500–1650* (Cologne, 1974).

[22] Garrett Mattingly, *Renaissance Diplomacy* (London, 1955).

[23] M. van Durme, *El cardenal Granvela (1517–1586). Imperio y revolución bajo Carlos V y Felipe II* (Barcelona, 1957).

[24] De Lamar Jensen, *Diplomacy and Dogmatism* (Cambridge, Mass., 1964).

[25] J. H. Elliott, *The Count-Duke of Olivares* (Yale University Press, 1986) is largely dedicated to foreign policy. For interesting aspects of secret diplomacy in this period, see M. A. Echevarria Bacigalupe, *La diplomacia secreta en Flandes, 1598–1643* (Leioa, Vizcaya 1984).

[26] John Lynch, 'Philip II and the Papacy', *Transactions of the Royal Historical Society*, 5th series, ii (1961).

[27] William S. Maltby, *Alba. A biography of Fernando Alvarez de Toledo, Third Duke of Alba 1507–1582* (University of California, 1983).

[28] J. A. Maravall, *La oposición política bajo los Austrias* (Barcelona, 1972).

[29] H. R. Trevor-Roper, 'Spain and Europe, 1598–1621', in *The New Cambridge Modern History*, vol. VI, *The Decline of Spain and the Thirty Years War* (Cambridge, 1970).

[30] Peter Brightwell, 'The Spanish Origins of the Thirty Years War', *European Studies Review*, 9 (1979) 409–31.

[31] José Alcalá-Zamora y Queipo de Llano, *España, Flandes y el mar del norte, 1618–1639* (Barcelona, 1975). An earlier, important article by the same author is 'Velas y cañones en la política septentrional de Felipe II', *Jerónimo Zurita. Cuadernos de Historia*, 23–24 (1970–1).

[32] Jonathan Israel, 'A conflict of empires: Spain and the Netherlands, 1618–1648', *Past and Present*, 76 (1977) 34–74.

[33] See H. Kamen, 'La política exterior', *Historia General de España y América*, vol. VIII, Editorial Rialp (Madrid, 1986).

[34] Hugo de Schepper, 'La organización de las finanzas públicas en los Países Bajos reales, 1480–1700. Una reseña', *Cuadernos de Investigación Histórica* (Madrid), 8 (1984) 7–34.

[35] C. H. Carter, 'Belgian "autonomy" under the Archdukes, 1598–1621', *Journal of Modern History*, XXXVI (1964); Paul Janssens, 'L'échec des tentatives de soulèvement aux Pays-Bas sous Philippe IV (1621–1665)', *Revue d'Histoire Diplomatique*, 92 (1978) 110–29.

[36] Rosario Villari, *La rivolta antispagnola a Napoli. Le origini 1586–1647* (Bari, 1967); A. d'Ambrosio, *Masaniello. Rivoluzione e contrarivoluzione nel reame di Napoli (1647–1648)* (Milan, 1962); Giuseppe Galasso, *Napoli doppo Masaniello. Politica, cultura, società* (Naples, 1972).

[37] L. Ribot, *La revuelta antiespañola de Messina. Causas y antecedentes (1591–1674)* (Valladolid, 1982).

[38] J. H. Elliott, *The Revolt of the Catalans* (Cambridge, 1963); José Sanabre, *La acción de Francia en Cataluña en la pugna por la hegemonía en Europa, 1648–1659* (Barcelona, 1956).

[39] R. D. Hussey and J. S. Bromley, 'The Spanish empire under foreign pressures, 1688–1716', in *New Cambridge Modern History*, vol. VI (Cambridge, 1970).

[40] Alcalá-Zamora, 'Razón de estado y geoestrategia en la política italiana de Carlos II', *Boletín de la Real Academia de la Historia* (1976) 297–358.

[41] W. H. Prescott, *The Conquest of Mexico* (Boston, 1843).

[42] John Hemming, *The Conquest of the Incas* (London, 1970).

[43] L. Bethell (ed.), *The Cambridge History of Latin America*, 2 vols (Cambridge, 1985).

The Peninsular Economy

[44] Earl J. Hamilton, *American Treasure and the Price Revolution in Spain, 1501–1650* (Cambridge, Mass., 1934). See also Dennis Flynn, 'A new perspective on the Spanish price revolution: the monetary approach

to the balance of payments', *Explorations in Economic History*, 15 (Oct. 1978) 388–406.

[45] For re-exports see Artur Attman, *Dutch Enterprise in the World Bullion Trade 1550–1800* (Göteborg, 1983); also his *American Bullion in the European World Trade 1600–1800* (Göteborg, 1986).

[46] Earl J. Hamilton, *War and Prices in Spain 1651–1800* (Cambridge, Mass., 1947), is the standard work on this period.

[47] Jordi Nadal, *La población española (siglos XVI a XX)* (Barcelona, 1984).

[48] Angel García Sanz, *Desarrollo y crisis del Antiguo Régimen en Castilla la Vieja. Economía y Sociedad en tierras de Segovia 1500–1814* (Madrid, 1977); Bartolomé Bennassar, *Valladolid au siècle d'or* (Paris, 1967).

[49] See Enrique Otte, 'Sevilla, plaza bancaria europea en el siglo XVI', in A. Otazu (ed.), *Dinero y Crédito (siglos XVI al XIX)*. *Actas del I Coloquio internacional de historia económia, Madrid–Segovia 1977* (Madrid, 1978).

[50] Annie Molinié-Bertrand, *Au Siècle d'or. L'Espagne et ses hommes. La Population du royaume de Castille au XVIe siècle* (Paris, 1985).

[51] Alberto Marcos Martín, *Auge y declive de un núcleo mercantil y financiero de Castilla la Vieja. Evolución demográfica de Medina del Campo durante los siglos XVI y XVII* (Valladolid, 1978).

[52] M. Weisser, 'The Decline of Castile Revisited: the Case of Toledo', *Journal of European Economic History*, 2 (1973) 614–40.

[53] Vicente Pérez Moreda, *Las crisis de mortalidad en la España interior (siglos XVI–XIX)* (Madrid, 1980). For the Mediterranean coast, there are data in N. Biraben, *Les Hommes et la peste en France et dans les pays européens et méditerranéens*, 2 vols (Paris, 1975).

[54] Henry Kamen, *Spain in the Later Seventeenth Century, 1665–1700* (London, 1980).

[55] José Manuel Pérez García, *Un modelo de sociedad rural de Antiguo Régimen en la Galicia costera: la Península del Salnés* (Santiago, 1979).

[56] James Casey, 'Spain: a Failed Transition', in Peter Clark (ed.) *The European Crisis of the 1590s* (London, 1985). An unsuccessful attempt to make population responsible for everything that went wrong in the peninsula ('the model that best explains the economy of early modern Spain is a Malthusian one') can be found in Carla Rahn Phillips, 'Time and Duration: A Model for the Economy of Early Modern Spain', *American Historical Review* (Sept. 1987).

[57] J. H. Elliott, 'Self-perception and decline in early seventeenth-century Spain', *Past and Present*, 74 (1977).

[58] Jordi Nadal and Emili Giralt, *La population catalane de 1553 à 1717: l'immigration française* (Paris, 1960); also Jordi Nadal, 'La població catalana als segles XVI i XVII', in *Historia de Catalunya*, vol. IV, Salvat editores (Barcelona, 1978).

[59] For example, J. E. Gelabert González, *Santiago y la tierra de Santiago de 1500 a 1640* (La Coruña, 1982). Another recent survey of Galicia is Pegerto Saavedra, *Economía, Política y Sociedad en Galicia: la provincia de Mondoñedo, 1480–1830* (Madrid, 1985).

[60] Among the several studies of the 1561 census, see B. Bennassar, 'Economie et société à Ségovie au milieu du XVIe siècle', *Anuario de*

Historia Económica y Social, I, i (1968); L. Martz and J. Porres, Toledo y los toledanos en 1561 (Toledo, 1974).

[61] Robert Rowland, 'Sistemas matrimoniales en la península ibérica (siglos XVI–XIX): una perspectiva regional', in V. Pérez Moreda and D. S. Reher (eds.) La Demografía Histórica de la Península Ibérica (Actas de las I Jornadas de Demografía Histórica, Madrid, Dec. 1983) (Madrid, 1986). For some aspects of the function of love, A. Redondo (ed.), Amours légitimes, amours illégitimes en Espagne (XVIe–XVIIe siècles) (Paris, 1985). See also J. Casey, 'La familia en la Andalucia del Antiguo Régimen', Historia 16, 57 (Jan. 1981).

[62] James Casey, The Kingdom of Valencia in the Seventeenth Century (Cambridge, 1979). In the useful collection of essays by James Casey and others, La Familia en la España Mediterránea (siglos XV–XIX) (Barcelona, 1987), Casey gives a good survey of the family in Andalucia.

[63] Bartolomé Bennassar, Recherches sur les grandes épidémies dans le Nord de l'Espagne à la fin du XVIe siècle (Paris, 1969).

[64] Antonio Dominguez Ortiz, La sociedad española en el siglo XVII, 2 vols (Madrid, 1963, 1970).

[65] Magnus Mörner, 'Spanish migration to the New World prior to 1810', in F. Chiapelli (ed.), First Images of America. The Impact of the New World on the Old, 2 vols (Los Angeles and London, 1976), vol. 2, 737–82; the same volume also contains P. Boyd-Bowman, 'Spanish emigrants to the Indies, 1595–98', 723–36. See also the latter's 'Patterns of emigration to the Indies until 1600', Hispanic American Historical Review, 56, iv (1976).

[66] Henry Kamen, 'The Mediterranean and the Expulsion of Spanish Jews in 1492', Past and Present 119 (May 1988).

[67] Antonio Domínguez Ortiz and Bernard Vincent, Historia de los Moriscos (Madrid, 1978); Henri Lapeyre, La Géographie de l'Espagne morisque (Paris, 1959). In English the best, albeit old, survey is still H. C. Lea, The Moriscos of Spain (London, 1901). The bibliography on the Granada Moriscos has been surveyed by M. Barrios Aguilera and M. M. Birriel Salcedo, La repoblación del reino de Granada después de la expulsión de los moriscos. Fuentes y bibliografía (Granada, 1986). There are useful perspectives in the collective volume Les Morisques et leurs temps (CNRS, Paris, 1983).

[68] James Casey, 'Moriscos and the Depopulation of Valencia', Past and Present, 50 (1971); and his important 'La situación económica de la nobleza valenciana en visperas de la expulsión de los Moriscos', in Homenaje al Dr D. Juan Reglà, 2 vols (Valencia, 1975), I, 515–25.

[69] Angel Rodríguez Sánchez, Cáceres: población y comportamientos demográficos en el siglo XVI (Cáceres, 1977).

[70] Gonzalo Anés, Las crisis agrarias en la España Moderna (Madrid, 1970).

[71] J. López Salazar and M. Martín Galán, 'Producción de cereales en Toledo, 1463–1690', Cuadernos de Historia Moderna y Contemporánea (Madrid), II (1981). The trend was similar in Andalucia: see Pierre Ponsot, 'La dîme, source d'histoire rurale et urbaine', Actas II Coloquios Historia de Andalucia, Nov. 1980. Andalucia Moderna, tomo I (Córdoba, 1983) pp. 353–62.

[72] Baudilio Barreiro, 'La introducción de nuevos cultivos y la evolución de la ganadería en Asturias durante la Edad Moderna', *Congreso de Historia Rural. Siglos XV al XIX* (Madrid, 1984) pp. 287–318; J. M. Pérez García, 'Aproximación al estudio de la penetración del maiz en Galicia', in A. Eiras Roel (ed.), *La Historia Social de Galicia en sus fuentes de protocolos* (Santiago, 1981) pp. 117–59.

[73] David E. Vassberg, 'The *tierras baldías*: community property and public lands in 16th century Castile', *Agricultural History*, 48, no. 3 (1974); 'The sale of *tierras baldías* in sixteenth-century Castile', *Journal of Modern History*, 47, no. 4 (1975).

[74] Gonzalo Anés, 'Tendencias de la producción agrícola en tierras de la Corona de Castilla (siglos XVI a XIX)', *Hacienda Pública Española*, no. 55 (1978) 97–111.

[75] Carmelo Viñas y Mey, *El problema de la tierra en la España de los siglos XVI–XVIII* (Madrid, 1941).

[76] Jesús García Fernández, 'Champs ouverts et champs clôturés en Vieille Castille', *Annales E.S.C.*, 20, no. 4 (1965) 692–718.

[77] David E. Vassberg, *Land and Society in Golden Age Castile* (Cambridge, 1984).

[78] Francis Brumont, *La Bureba à l'époque de Philippe II* (New York, 1977). To be supplemented by his 'La rente de la terre en Rioja occidentale à l'époque moderne', *Mélanges de la Casa de Velázquez*, xvi (1980) 237–72.

[79] Noël Salomon, *La Campagne de Nouvelle Castille à la fin du XVIe siècle d'après les 'Relaciones Topográficas'* (Paris, 1964).

[80] Eva Serra, 'El règim feudal català abans i després de la sentència arbitral de Guadalupe', *Recerques*, 10 (1980). See also the group of essays in the *Revista de Girona*, xxxii, no. 118 (Sept–Oct 1986).

[81] The classic study is Julius Klein, *The Mesta. A study in Spanish economic history 1273–1836* (Harvard, 1920). Recent studies include Felipe Ruiz Martín, 'Pastos y ganaderos en Castilla: La Mesta, 1450–1600', in M. Spallanzini (ed.), *La lana come materia prima* (Florence, 1974).

[82] Paulino Iradiel Murugarren, *Evolución de la industria textil castellana en los siglos XIII–XVI. Factores de desarrollo, organización y costes de la producción manufacturera en Cuenca* (Salamanca, 1974). On the problems of textiles in the subsequent period see J. I. Fortea Pérez, *Córdoba en el siglo XVI: las bases demográficas ye económicas de una expansión urbana* (Córdoba, 1981). For a useful general perspective of the economy, see V. Vásquez de Prada, *Historia Económica y Social de España*, vol. iii: *Los Siglos XVI y XVII* (Madrid, 1978).

[83] Carla Rahn Phillips, 'The Spanish Wool Trade, 1500–1780', *Journal of Economic History*, xlii, 4 (Dec. 1982) 774–94; and her 'Spanish merchants and the wool trade in the sixteenth century', *Sixteenth-Century Journal*, xiv, 3 (1983) 259–82. For the later period, Jonathan Israel, 'Spanish wool exports and the European economy, 1610–1640', *Economic History Review*, xxxiii, 2 (1980).

[84] Henri Lapeyre, *Une famille de marchands: les Ruiz. Contribution à l'étude*

du commerce entre la France et l'Espagne au temps de Philippe II (Paris, 1955).

[85] José Gentil da Silva, *En Espagne. Développement économique, subsistance, déclin* (Paris, 1965), has interesting data on the points in the peninsula to which bullion went.

[86] Pierre Chaunu, *Séville et l'Amérique XVIe–XVIIe siècle* (Paris, 1977), is a condensation of the earlier major work: *Séville et l'Atlantique* (1504–1650), 8 vols (Paris, 1955–60).

[87] A. M. Bernal, A. Collantes de Terán, and A. García-Baquero, 'Sevilla: de los gremios a la industrialización', *Estudios de Historia Social*, no. 5–6 (1978).

[88] A. Girard, *Le commerce français à Séville et Cadiz au temps des Habsbourg* (Paris, 1932); J. Everaert, *De internationale en koloniale Handel der Vlaamse Firma's te Cadiz 1670–1700* (Bruges, 1973).

[89] David R. Ringrose, *Madrid and the Spanish Economy 1560–1850* (University of California, 1983).

[90] M. Morineau, *Incroyables gazettes et fabuleux métaux. Les retours des trésors américains d'après les gazettes hollandaises (XVIe–XVIIIe siècles)* (Paris, 1985).

[91] P. Molas Ribalta, 'A tres-cents anys del "Fénix de Cataluña". Recuperació i reformisme sota Carles II', *Pedralbes* (Barcelona), 3 (1983) 147–174.

[92] P. J. Pla Alberola, *La población del marquesado de Guadalest en el siglo XVII* (Alicante, 1983). For a good survey of the impact of crisis on one community, J. Casey, 'Tierra y Sociedad en Castellon de la Plana, 1608–1702', *Estudis*, 7 (1980) 13–46.

[93] H. Kamen, 'The decline of Castile: the last crisis', *Economic History Review*, xvii i (1964) 63–76.

[94] P. Molas Ribalta, 'La Junta de Comercio de Barcelona', *Anuario de Historia Económica y Social*, 3 (1970) 235–79.

[95] P. Molas Ribalta, *La burguesía mercantil en la España del Antiguo Régimen* (Madrid, 1985). This has an excellent up-to-date bibliography.

[96] José Antonio Maravall, *Estado Moderno y Mentalidad Social, siglos XV a XVII*, 2 vols (Madrid, 1972).

[97] William D. Phillips, 'The Castilian community in sixteenth-century Bruges', *Sixteenth-Century Journal*, xvii, 1 (1986). See also note 139 below.

Political Evolution

[98] Francisco Tomás y Valiente, *Manual de Historia del Derecho Español* (Madrid, 1979), part iv.

[99] J. Vicens Vives, 'The administrative structure of the state in the sixteenth and seventeenth centuries', in Henry J. Cohn (ed.), *Government in Reformation Europe 1520–1560* (London, 1971).

[100] José Antonio Maravall, 'The Origins of the Modern State', *Journal of World History*, vi (1961). There are few surveys of the pre-eighteenth-

century administration; for a perspective, see P. Molas, 'La historia social de la administración española. Balance y perspectivas para el siglo XVIII', *Cuadernos de Investigación Histórica*, 6 (1982) 151–68.

[101] See Map 5 in Kamen, *Spain 1469–1714*.

[102] José Antonio Escudero, *Los secretarios de Estado y de Despacho, 1474–1724*, 4 vols (Madrid, 1976). For a summary of its conclusions, J. Mercader Riba, 'Los secretarios reales en la Historia de la Administración española', *Hispania*, 117 (1971). On the Council of State, see now Feliciano Barrios, *El Consejo de Estado de la monarquía española, 1521–1812* (Madrid, 1984).

[103] Richard L. Kagan, *Students and Society in Early Modern Spain* (Baltimore, 1974). Among recent studies of the higher education system, see L. E. Rodríguez-San Pedro Bezares, *La Universidad Salmantina del Barroco, 1598–1625*, 3 vols (Salamanca, 1986).

[104] Jean-Marc Pelorson, *Les 'letrados': juristes castillans sous Philippe III* (Poitiers, 1980); I. A. A. Thompson, 'The Rule of the Law in Early Modern Castile', *European History Quarterly*, 14 (1984).

[105] Janine Fayard, *Les membres du Conseil de Castille à l'époque moderne (1621–1746)* (Paris–Geneva, 1979).

[106] Hayward Keniston, *Francisco de los Cobos, secretary of the emperor Charles V* (Pittsburgh, 1960). On Charles' key adviser Gattinara, see John M. Headley, *The Emperor and his Chancellor* (Cambridge, 1983).

[107] Gregorio Marañón, *Antonio Pérez* (London, 1954).

[108] Francisco Tomás y Valiente, *Los validos en la monarquía española del siglo XVII* (Madrid, 1963).

[109] Patrick Williams, 'Philip III and the restoration of Spanish government, 1598–1603', *English Historical Review*, 88 (1973).

[110] Benjamin González Alonso, *El corregidor castellano (1348–1808)* (Madrid, 1970); the same author looks at aspects of local government in *Sobre el Estado y la Administración de la Corona de Castilla en el Antiguo Régimen* (Madrid, 1981). A recent short study is Marvin Lunenfeld, *Keepers of the City. The corregidores of Isabella of Castile (1474–1504)* (Cambridge, 1987).

[111] H. Kamen, 'El establecimiento de los intendentes en la administración española', *Hispania*, 95 (1964).

[112] J. Lalinde Abadía, *La institución virreinal en Cataluña, 1471–1716* (Barcelona, 1964).

[113] This is despite urban studies such as F. Chacón Jiménez, *Murcia en la centuria del quinientos* (Murcia, 1979), and C. Rahn Phillips, *Ciudad Real 1500–1750* (Harvard, 1979). For cities in general, see the composite work *La Ciudad Hispánica durante los siglos XIII al XVI*, 2 vols (University of Madrid, 1985).

[114] M. A. Ladero Quesada, 'Les finances royales de Castille à la veille des temps modernes', *Annales ESC*, 25, iii (1970).

[115] Miguel Artola, *La Hacienda del Antiguo Régimen* (Madrid, 1982). For the evolution of *juros*, Alvaro Castillo Pintado, 'Dette flottante et dette consolidée en Espagne de 1559 à 1600', *Annales ESC*, 11 (1963).

[116] Margarita Cuartas Rivero, 'La venta de oficios públicos en el siglo

XVI', *Actas del IV Symposium de Historia de la Administración* (Madrid, 1983) pp. 225–260; also her 'La venta de oficios públicos en Castilla-León en el siglo XVI', *Hispania*, XLIV, 158 (1984) 495–516.

[117] Antonio Domínguez Ortiz, 'La venta de cargos y oficios públicos en Castilla y sus consecuencias económicas y sociales', *Anuario de Historia Económica y Social*, 3 (1970).

[118] I. A. A. Thompson, 'Crown and Cortes in Castile, 1590–1665', *Parliaments, Estates and Representation*, II, i (June 1982) 29–45. See also Charles Jago, 'Habsburg absolutism and the Cortes of Castile', *American Historical Review*, 86 (2) (April 1981); and his 'Philip II and the Cortes of 1576', *Past and Present*, 109 (1985).

[119] G. Colas Latorre and J. A. Salas Ausens, *Aragón bajo los Austrias* (Saragossa, 1977).

[120] Jesús Lalinde Abadía, 'El sistema normativo navarro', *Anuario de Historia del Derecho Español*, 40 (1970) 85–108.

[121] The administrative independence of the northern provinces may be seen for example by consulting E. J. de Labayru, *Historia General del Señorío de Bizcaya*, 6 vols (Bilbao–Madrid, 1895–1901); Gregorio Monreal, *Las instituciones públicas del señorío de Vizcaya* (Bilbao, 1974); E. Fernández Villamil, *Juntas del Reino de Galicia*, 3 vols (Madrid, 1962).

[122] Cf. Carmelo Lisón Tolosana, *Belmonte de los Caballeros. A Sociological Study of a Spanish Town* (Oxford, 1966).

[123] Cf. John B. Owens, *Rebelión, Monarquía y Oligarquía Murciana en la época de Carlos V* (Murcia, 1980).

[124] Jean Vilar, *Literatura y economía: la figura satírica del arbitrista en el Siglo de Oro* (Madrid, 1973).

[125] Cf. J. A. Fernández Santamaría, *Reason of State and Statecraft in Spanish Political Thought, 1595–1640* (New York, 1983).

[126] Cited by Luciano Pereña in his edition of Francisco Suárez, *De juramento fidelitatis*, 2 vols (Madrid, 1979).

[127] Jean Vilar, 'Formes et tendances de l'opposition sous Olivares: Lisón y Biedma, *Defensor de la Patria*', *Mélanges de la Casa de Velázquez*, 7 (1971) 263–294.

[128] Joseph Pérez, *La révolution des 'Comunidades' de Castille (1520–1521)* (Bordeaux, 1970); J. A. Maravall, *Las Comunidades de Castilla: una primera revolución moderna* (Madrid, 1979); Stephen Haliczer, *The Comuneros of Castile. The Forging of a Revolution, 1475–1521* (Madison, 1981); E. Durán, *Les Germanies als Països Catalans* (Barcelona, 1982).

[129] J. I. Gutiérrez Nieto, *Las comunidades como movimiento antiseñorial* (Barcelona, 1973).

[130] Sebastián García Martínez, *Bandolerismo, piratería y control de moriscos en Valencia durante el reinado de Felipe II* (Valencia, 1977).

[131] A. Domínguez Ortiz, *Alteraciones andaluzas* (Madrid, 1973).

[132] H. Kamen, 'A forgotten insurrection of the seventeenth century: the Catalan peasant rising of 1688', *Journal of Modern History*, 49 (1977); for the 1693 rising, S. García Martínez, 'En torno a los problemas

del campo en el sur del reino de Valencia', *VIII Congreso de Historia de la Corona de Aragón*, vol. IV, 215–234.

[133] Jordi Vidal Pla, *Guerra dels segadors i crisi social. Els exiliats filipistes (1640–1652)* (Barcelona, 1984).

[134] Fernando Sánchez Marcos, *Cataluña y el Gobierno central tras la Guerra de los Segadores 1652–1679* (Barcelona, 1983).

[135] Pierre Vilar, *Le 'Manual de la Companya Nova' de Gibraltar, 1709–1723* (Paris, 1962); Joaquim Llovet, *Mataró, 1680–1719: el pas de vila a ciutat* (Mataró, 1966).

[136] J. M. Torras i Ribé, 'Reflexions sobre l'actitud dels pobles i estaments catalans durant la guerra de Successió', *Pedralbes*, 1 (1981) 187–209; See also Nuria Sales, *Els botiflers, 1705–1714* (Barcelona, 1981).

[137] The best general survey of early eighteenth-century Spain is in A. Domínguez Ortiz, *Sociedad y Estado en el siglo XVIII español* (Barcelona, 1976).

Society and Culture

[138] The pioneer in anthropological studies was Julio Caro Baroja; highly influential has been Julian Pitt-Rivers, *The People of the Sierra*, 2nd edn (Chicago, 1971).

[139] Fundamental is J. A. Goris, *Etudes sur les colonies marchandes méridionales (Portugais, Espagnols, Italiens) à Anvers de 1488 à 1567* (Louvain, 1925).

[140] Cf. Robert S. Lopez, 'Market expansion: the case of Genoa', *Journal of Economic History*, XXIV (1964) 445–64. On Spanish–Italian trade, Felipe Ruiz Martín, *Lettres marchandes échangées entre Florence et Medina del Campo* (Paris, 1965).

[141] Paul Hiltpold, 'Noble status and urban privilege: Burgos 1572', *Sixteenth-Century Journal*, XII, 4 (1981) 21–44; James Amelang, *Honored Citizens of Barcelona. Patrician culture and class relations, 1490–1714* (Princeton, 1986).

[142] W. Callahan, *Honor, Commerce and Industry in Eighteenth-Century Spain* (Boston, 1972).

[143] Marie-Claude Gerbet, *La noblesse dans le royaume de Castille. Etude sur ses structures sociales en Estrémadure (1454–1516)* (Paris, 1979). For the military orders, L. P. Wright, 'The military orders in sixteenth- and seventeenth-century Spanish society', *Past and Present*, 43 (1969).

[144] I. A. A. Thompson, 'Neo-noble nobility: concepts of *hidalguía* in early modern Castile', *European History Quarterly*, 15 (1985) 379–406.

[145] Ibid., 'The purchase of nobility in Castile, 1552–1700', *Journal of European Economic History*, 8, ii (1979).

[146] The great Mendoza family is an exception. They have been studied in their context, C. Arteaga, *La Casa del Infantado* (Madrid, 1944), and in their culture, Helen Nader, *The Mendoza family in the Spanish renaissance* (New Brunswick, 1979).

[147] For jurisdictions in Castile, see Miguel Artola (ed.), *La España del Antiguo Régimen: Salamanca* (Salamanca, 1966); *Castilla la Vieja* (1967); *Castilla la Nueva y Extremadura* (1971). For *señoríos*, Salvador Moxó,

'Los señoríos. En torno a una problemática para el estudio del régimen señorial', *Hispania*, 94 (1964).

[148] Helen Nader, 'Noble income in 16th century Castile: the case of the Marquises of Mondéjar', *Economic History Review*, xxx (1977) 411–428; C. Jago, 'The Crisis of the Aristocracy in seventeenth-century Castile', *Past and Present*, 84 (1979). For the evolution of noble rents in Catalonia, Montserrat Durán, 'L'evolució de l'ingrés senyorial a Catalunya (1500–1799)', *Recerques*, 17 (1985) 7–42.

[149] J. López-Salazar Pérez, 'Una empresa agraria capitalista en la Castilla del XVII: la Hacienda de D. Gonzalo Muñoz Treviño de Loaisa', *Hispania*, 148 (1981) 355–407.

[150] Alberto Marcos Martín, *Economía, sociedad, pobreza en Castilla: Palencia 1500–1814*, 2 vols (Palencia, 1985). For another perspective, Claude Larquié, 'Une approche quantitative de la pauvreté: les madrilènes et la mort au XVIIe siècle', *Annales de Démographie historique* (1978).

[151] Linda Martz, *Poverty and Welfare in Habsburg Spain. The example of Toledo* (Cambridge, 1983). Work done for the poor by confraternities is described by Maureen Flynn, 'Charitable ritual in late medieval and early modern Spain', *Sixteenth-Century Journal*, 16, no. 3 (1985); and by W. J. Callahan, 'Corporate charity in Spain: the Hermandad del Refugio of Madrid, 1618–1814', *Histoire Sociale*, 9 (1976) 159–86.

[152] J. A. Maravall, *La literatura picaresca desde la historia social* (Madrid, 1986), the last work of a great historian. On some aspects of crime, see R. Pike, 'Crime and punishment in sixteenth-century Spain', *Journal of Economic History*, 3 (1976) 699–904, and H. Kamen, 'Public authority and popular crime. Banditry in Valencia 1660–1714', *Journal of European Economic History*, 3, iii (1974) 654–87.

[153] For some English views, see Patricia Shaw Fairman, *España vista por los Ingleses del siglo XVII* (Madrid, 1981).

[154] On Spanish culture in Italy, there is a short summary by Franco Meregalli, *Presenza della letteratura spagnola in Italia* (Florence, 1974). See also A. Rochon (ed.), *Présence et influence de l'Espagne dans la culture italienne de la renaissance* (Paris, 1978).

[155] For the Netherlands, see e.g. Geoffrey Parker, 'New light on an old theme: Spain and the Netherlands 1550–1650', *European History Quarterly*, 15, no. 2 (April 1985) 219–37.

[156] Asensio Gutiérrez, *La France et les français dans la littérature espagnole. Un aspect de la xénophobie en Espagne (1598–1665)* (St Etienne, 1977).

[157] Christian Péligry, 'Les éditeurs lyonnais et le marché espagnol aux XVIe et XVIIe siècles', in *Livre et Lecture en Espagne et en France sous l'Ancien Régime. Colloque de la Casa de Velázquez* (Paris, 1981).

[158] Virgilio Pinto Crespo, *Inquisición y control ideológico en la España del siglo XVI* (Madrid, 1983).

[159] Antonio Márquez, *Literatura e Inquisición en España, 1478–1834* (Madrid, 1980).

[160] Antonio Márquez, *Los Alumbrados. Orígenes y filosofía (1525–1559)* (Madrid, 1980); Angela Selke, *El Santo Oficio de la Inquisición. Proceso de Fr. Francisco Ortiz* (Madrid, 1968).

[161] Marcel Bataillon, *Erasme et l'Espagne* (Paris, 1937).

[162] H. Kamen, 'Toleration and Dissent in Sixteenth-Century Spain: the Alternative Tradition', *Sixteenth-Century Journal*, 18, no. 4 (1987).

[163] A recent bibliography is Gordon Kinder, *Spanish Protestants and Reformers in the Sixteenth Century* (London, 1983). For some perspectives, J. E. Longhurst, 'Luther in Spain 1520–1540', *Proceedings of the American Philosophical Society*, 103 (1959) 66–93; A. Redondo, 'Luther et l'Espagne de 1520 à 1536', *Mélanges de la Casa de Velázquez*, 1 (1965); Carlos Gilly, *Spanien und der Basler Buchdruck bis 1600* (Basel and Frankfurt, 1985), Chap. 5: 'Die Häretiker'.

[164] The standard history is Henry Charles Lea, *A History of the Inquisition of Spain*, 4 vols (New York, 1906–1908). The modern general survey by Henry Kamen, *Inquisition and Society in Spain in the Sixteenth and Seventeenth Centuries* (London and Bloomington, 1985), has a bibliography of recent work.

[165] See the chapter by J. Contreras in G. Henningsen and J. Tedeschi (eds), *The Inquisition in Early Modern Europe: Studies in Sources and Methods* (De Kalb, Illinois, 1986).

[166] For some recent social perspectives, Jaime Contreras, *El Santo Oficio de la Inquisición de Galicia* (Madrid, 1982); J.-P. Dedieu, 'The Inquisition and Popular Culture in New Castile', in S. Haliczer (ed.), *Inquisition and Society in Early Modern Europe* (London, 1986).

[167] On its anti-semitic activities, recent studies include Haim Beinart, *Conversos on Trial. The Inquisition in Ciudad Real* (Jerusalem, 1981); on its anti-Islamic activities, see e.g. Anwar G. Chejne, *Islam and the West: the Moriscos* (New York, Albany, 1983); Louis Cardaillac, *Morisques et Chrétiens. Un affrontement polémique (1492–1640)* (Paris, 1977).

[168] H. Kamen, 'Una crisis de conciencia en la España del Siglo de Oro: la Inquisición contra la *limpieza de sangre*', *Bulletin Hispanique* 88 (1986), no. 3–4.

[169] There is a useful short essay by J. L. González Novalín on 'Religiosidad y reforma del pueblo cristiano', in Ricardo García-Villoslada (ed.), *Historia de la Iglesia en España*, vol. III, part 1 (Madrid, 1980), pp. 351–84.

[170] William A. Christian Jr., *Local Religion in Sixteenth-century Spain* (Princeton, 1981); *Apparitions in late medieval and Renaissance Spain* (Princeton, 1981).

[171] Gustav Henningsen, *The Witches' Advocate. Basque Witchcraft and the Spanish Inquisition* (Reno, 1980).

[172] Most notably in his masterpiece, *Historia de los Heterodoxos Españoles*, first published in 1880.

[173] B. Bennassar, *L'Homme espagnol. Attitudes et mentalités du XVIe au XIXe siècle* (Paris, 1975).

[174] This does not, of course, detract from the important contribution of Otis H. Green, *Spain and the Western Tradition: The Castilian Mind in Literature from El Cid to Calderón*, 4 vols (Madison, 1963–6).

[175] J. M. Diez Borque, *Sociología de la comedia española del siglo XVII* (Madrid, 1976); J. A. Maravall, *La Cultura del Barroco* (Madrid, 1975); J. Caro Baroja, *El Carnaval* (Madrid, 1979).

Glossary

alumbrados. Illuminists, groups of mystics who minimised the role of the Church and of ceremonies.

arbitristas. Writers who drew up *arbitrios* or proposals for economic and political reform.

carrera de Indias. The trading voyage to and from America.

censo. Annuity drawn from loans made to individuals or public bodies; there were various types of *censos*.

chancillerías. Term applied to the Castilian high courts in Valladolid and Granada.

ciutadans honrats. 'Honoured citizens', the highest civic rank, equal to nobility, granted by major towns in the Crown of Aragon, especially Barcelona.

Comunidades. The urban 'communities' of Castile, especially those who took part in the revolts of 1520; the persons taking part were *Comuneros*.

concejo abierto. 'Open council', the governing body of many towns and villages in Castile.

conversos. Term applied particularly to Christianised Jews.

corregidores. Crown-appointed civil governors in main Castilian towns.

Diputación. Standing committee of the Cortes, with members appointed from each estate. In Barcelona the *Diputación* was also called the *Generalitat*.

fueros. Local laws and privileges, usually applied to the non-Castilian parts of Spain.

hidalgo. One having the status of nobility (*hidalguía*), but without denoting rank.

juros. Annuities paid out of state income for loans to the crown.

letrados. University graduate in law, basis of the state bureaucracy.

limpieza de sangre. 'Purity of blood', freedom from taint of Jewish blood.

mayorazgo. Entail, settlement restricting the alienation of or succession to a noble estate.

Mesta. Castilian guild of sheep-owners.

pecheros. Commoners, tax-payers.

regidor. Town councillor.

servicios. A 'service' or grant of taxes made by the Castilian Cortes.

valido. Chief minister or 'favourite' in royal government.

Index